MULTIPLY

DIVIDE

On the American Real and Surreal

wendy s. walters

Sarabande  Books
LOUISVILLE, KENTUCKY

Managing Editor
Sarabande Books, Inc.
2234 Dundee Road, Suite 200
Louisville, KY 40205

Library of Congress Cataloging-in-Publication Data

Walters, Wendy S.
[Essays. Selections]
Multiply/divide : on the American real and surreal / Wendy S. Walters.
   pages cm
 Includes bibliographical references and index.
 ISBN 978-1-941411-04-9 (paperback)
1. City and town life–United States–21st century. 2. United States–Social
conditions–21st century. 3. United States–Race relations–21st century.
4. Sex discrimination–United States–21st century. I. Title. II. Title: American real and surreal.
 E169.12W343 2015
 306.097309'05——dc23

2014047727

Cover by Kristen Radtke.
Interior by Kirkby Gann Tittle.
Manufactured in Canada.
This book is printed on acid-free paper.
Sarabande Books is a nonprofit literary organization.

 The Kentucky Arts Council, the state arts agency, supports
Sarabande Books with state tax dollars and federal funding
from the National Endowment for the Arts.

 This project is supported in part by an award from the
National Endowment for the Arts.

CONTENTS

Author's Note	*v*
Lonely in America	1
Chicago Radio	33
Cleveland	45
Manhattanville, Part One	57
In Search of the Face	69
Multiply/Divide	89
The Personal	95
Post-Logical Notes on Self-Election	107
Cowboy Horizon	131
Procedural	141
Manhattanville, Part Two	153
When the Sea Comes for Us	179
Norway	195
Acknowledgments	*203*
The Author	*205*

Author's Note

The subtitle of this book—*On the American Real and Surreal*—marks an important distinction. Some of the essays herein are based entirely on fact: carefully reported and researched, they stand as nonfiction. Others are works of fiction. Some are a mix of the two. To avoid confusion, I have noted below the genres of each work in the collection.

"Lonely in America," "Manhattanville, Part One," "Manhattanville, Part Two," "The Personal," and "When The Sea Comes for Us" should be considered nonfiction as they are works of reportage and/or memoir.

"Cleveland," "Multiply/Divide," "Cowboy Horizon," "In Search of the Face," and "Norway" are fictional scenarios that, in some cases, are based on characters and events from history and/or the present.

"Chicago Radio" and "Post-logical Notes on Self-Election" are lyric essays—a form that blends poetry and prose, memoir and reportage, actual and imagined events—with the goal of making an argument.

I make the above categorizations because I think they are important. But I also make them with a bit of pause, because the border between nonfiction and fiction—while seemingly clear as black and white—is often porous enough to render the distinction irrelevant. Take, as a hypothetical example, the writer who pens a memoir about a life with her parents, but leaves out the complicated relationship with her siblings, omitting for the reader a complete understanding of her family dynamic. Her memoir is "nonfiction." But that doesn't make it true. Conversely many works of fiction, precisely because they take liberties with fact, can depict a world that is better designed than our own to reveal truth. One could make a similar case about the distinction between the surreal and the real.

These works are my attempt to address such nuances as they unfold place by place, argument by argument, and story by story.

Wendy S. Walters
December 2014
New York, NY

Lonely in America

I HAVE NEVER BEEN particularly interested in slavery, perhaps because it is such an obvious fact of my family's history. We know where we were enslaved in America, but we don't know much else about our specific conditions. The fact that I am descended from slaves is hard to acknowledge on a day-to-day basis, because slavery does not fit with my self-image. Perhaps this is because I am pretty certain I would not have survived it. I am naturally sharp-tongued, suffer from immobility when I am cold, and am susceptible to terrible sinus infections and allergies. My eyesight is poor. Most of the time I don't think about how soft the good fortune of freedom has made me, but if I were to quantify my weaknesses of body and character I would guess that at least half the fortitude my enslaved ancestors must have possessed has been lost with each generation in the family line, leaving me with little more than an obtuse and metaphorical relationship to that sort of suffering.

I resist thinking about slavery because I want to avoid the overwhelming feeling that comes from trying to conceive of the terror, violence, and indignity of it. I do not like to think of it happening in my hometown, where I work, in my neighborhood, or near any of the places where I conduct my life. My cultural memory of slavery, which I don't think is so unlike that of many other Americans, suggests that it was primarily a Southern phenomenon, one confined to the borders of plantations, which if they haven't been transformed into shopping complexes or subdivisions, exist now only as nostalgic, sentimentalized tourist attractions. The landscapes associated with slavery, however, extend far beyond the South.

My home is in New England and in the winter my house feels slight against the wind as its windows tremble with every blustery gust, which makes me want to stay in bed, though I am not at all the type of person who likes to linger there once awake, unless circumstances are such that I am not alone, and then, even in that rare case, I can be restless and ready to set forth at sunrise. In the winter of 2006, I was not working at my regular job, which might have been a good thing had I not been prone to a melancholy obsession over recent personal disappointments. I began to notice pains in my body I had never felt before: a tendon pulling across the length of my leg when I sat down, a sharp twinge in my side when I stood up, and sometimes when I'd shower my skin was so sore I could barely stand to feel the water on it. I knew these pains were likely psychosomatic, evidence of how deeply I was suffering from loneliness. Because I suspected that the hope of escaping my loneliness was adding to my discomfort, I had been trying to cure myself of optimism as a strategy to ward off future misery. The value of this approach was confirmed by a self-help book I kept on my nightstand. When I dared to open it, I could read only a single chapter at a sitting because each reiterated a simple point that I just could not seem to accept—that to become free from disappointment one must acknowledge the obvious, then learn to live with it.

By mid-January, the United States' war with Iraq was coming to the end of its fourth year, the war in Afghanistan was intensifying again, and the shortcomings of the federal government that had been noted

after Hurricane Katrina were fading from media attention, which was now absorbed with a surge of reports
that, come summer, another movie star couple would
be expecting their first biological child. I found myself
momentarily enthralled in speculation: how long would
this new relationship last? What did his ex-wife think of
the sudden pregnancy of his new girlfriend? Who would
take time off from their career to care for the family?
These questions, though deeply irrelevant to my own
life, served to distract me from the obvious fact that
an unpopular war, entered into on misinformation, was
showing no signs of ending. Every morning I studied the
news reports on the radio, which covered many subjects: planned highway construction projects, politics,
movie stars, pop music stars, television stars, impend-
ing diseases, lying politicians, local sports, bank rob-
beries, soldiers killed in Iraq. I suppose I was hoping the
radio would serve as a kind of personal oracle, that stories of real human struggle might release me from solip-
sistic self-pity and show me how to leave my bungalow
and enter the world with a sense of purpose, or at least
a sense of direction.

It was with this ambition that I had gone to New
Orleans to help my great aunt Louise come to recognize
that her home there had been destroyed, even though
my gumption was clearly tainted with dread. Sitting in

a cold house listening to the radio was painful enough, but the thought of actually walking through so much loss made me worry that I would have to face more of the obvious than I could be distracted from noticing. As our plane flew over the Gulf Coast it was hard to tell how bad things actually were on the ground. Muddy patches of brown and tan signaled the normally slow growth of a Southern winter. I saw the edge of Lake Pontchartrain into which, during the early 1920s, my great-grandmother Susie had thrown her wedding ring when she needed to affirm a point that her husband would not accept. On our descent I began to see blue tarps stretched over large holes in people's roofs.

When we arrived at Aunt Lou's tiny, red brick, rail-road-style house, her nephew met us. Chester was a former longshoreman. He had returned to the city a few weeks after the water had been pumped out and had been living in a FEMA trailer while he gutted his own house. Even though he had warned my mother and Aunt Lou on the phone that the house was in very bad condition, he wanted to make sure we understood this before we entered it, because from the outside, there appeared to be little structural damage. About four feet from the ground, a black, bathtub-ring-like watermark circled the exterior. Garbage and a broken ladder lay across the front lawn. When we opened the front door, dirt, mud, debris, and seaweed covered the hardwood floors and the sofa, which had floated over to the opposite wall from which it had been set. The house looked like someone had picked it up and shook it hard before returning it to its cinder-block frame. We put on face masks, gloves, and booties over our shoes. A chifforobe sitting in water for weeks had gently exploded and still-wet clothes poked out of holes in the sides. Black and brown mud blotted the wall next to an antique brass bed. In the back room, the ceiling had caved in and wires and other debris hung low from what was left of the roof, like snakes in trees.

Aunt Lou said, *My house is tore up.*

Radio and television news reports about New Orleans mentioned that several cemeteries had been badly damaged by the flooding, and Chester's wife said coffins had been turning up all over the city. So I convinced my mother to drive over to Holt Cemetery, where our family crypt is situated, but she wouldn't get out of the car to check on it with me. Instead she shouted from its window, *Watch out for water moccasins!* as I walked through a rusty and twisted wrought-iron fence bolstered by rotten tree stumps into a field of tall, dead grasses and sun-bleached tombstones. Cypress trees sheltered the perimeter, branches reaching like veins across a heart.

Despite the fact that most of the graves at Holt are below ground, unlike many cemeteries in New Orleans, it looked to me that Holt had kept hold of its dead better than the gravesites near the end of Canal Street, where mausoleums appeared stained and tumbled over by water. In the early 1900s a portion of Holt was used as a "pauper's field" for the poor and indigent, and during segregation it was one place where blacks could be buried. Our family crypt had been there longer than anyone could remember, but its precise location was unknown; its marker had been stolen in 1969, just weeks after my great-grandmother was laid to rest. Up close I could see new grass, slender and gold-green, appearing in short tufts at the foot of the headstones, most of which were pitched in one direction or another toward the ground. Handmade markers in wood or cement were adorned with bottle glass, sea shells or not at all, with the names and dates of the deceased written in by hand. Some had been decorated with Mardi Gras beads and silk flowers. I walked down the dirt path to the part of the cemetery where most of the stones were missing and called out to my ancestors. *I have no idea where you are. Tell me where you are.* But I heard nothing.

Ten years ago, when I last visited Holt, the grounds had not been well-tended, and even then many of the grave markers were missing, in disrepair, or toppled down. Back then I had only a piece of scrap paper with a row and plot number written on it to guide me to the crypt's location. The ground, which was deeply sunken where bodies were buried, looked as if waves were passing through it in slow motion. On that visit I worried that I could not read the names of the people I was walking over to apologize directly for the disrespect of having done so. Hastily I laid some flowers and a note where I thought the crypt should be and left without ever planning to return. On this visit, Holt felt strangely serene; unlike the rest of the city, it appeared not to have changed in any significant way. In fact, I might have wandered amongst the unknown dead for hours had I not heard my mother frantically shouting from the car: *Wendy, come on! We've got to get to Constantinople before dark!*

We picked up Aunt Lou from Chester's and drove over to Constantinople, a street in the Magazine district, to meet up with her childhood friend who had survived the flood trapped with her son in the attic of his house for a week before being rescued. Because none of the traffic lights were working, my mother was nervous and complained all the way there about how I had lingered too long in the cemetery. She chided me that one should let the dead rest. *That's right,* Aunt Lou said. I interrupted: *I just wanted to make sure that our people hadn't floated away.* They went quiet. *But I took a walk around, and it looked like everybody was still tucked in tight.*

I returned from New Orleans more miserable than when I left. As much as I had wanted to come back from that trip with a sense of conviction, inspired to action that would distract me from my loneliness, I could not find a singular source of outrage on which to fixate—not poverty, racism, the failure of the federal government, a history of community self-destructiveness, a river, a lake, or a hurricane. Not a house without a roof, a felled tree across a path, a tumbled-down tombstone, or a wayward corpse. I was faced with too much that was obvious about the way class and race work in America. More than I wanted to see. More than I was capable of seeing.

This is when I realized my loneliness had deeper roots than I had initially suspected, and that, in addition to personal disappointments, it came from having a profound sense of disconnection from what I thought America was, and who, in that context, I knew myself to be. My post-New Orleans loneliness seemed to emanate from a place that preceded my own memory and stretched across time into a future that extended far beyond my vision. It was as if I had been thrown overboard into the sea and was paralyzed by the shock of it. I could neither breathe nor drown. I could not sink or return to the surface.

Then early one morning in January as I was listening to Boston's public radio station, I heard a story about the 2003 discovery of a gravesite in Portsmouth, New Hampshire. As city workers attempted to dig a manhole near the corner of Court and Chestnut Streets in the seaside town, a pine coffin was discovered with leg bones sticking out. An independent archaeological firm had been brought in immediately to lead an exhumation. Eight coffins and the remains of thirteen people were removed. The report noted that a combination of forensic evidence and DNA testing had confirmed that at least four of the remains in question were of African ancestry, most likely slaves buried there during the 1700s. The archaeologists' report had just been released to the city of Portsmouth, which was engaged in public discussion about what was the most appropriate and respectful way to deal with those exhumed, as well as the fact that as many as two hundred people might still be buried at the site.

Perhaps if I had not already spent more than a couple of weeks being so down in the dumps, if talk about the expected duration of the wars in Iraq and Afghanistan suggested a time frame other than the interminable, if images from my trip to New Orleans were not so powerfully present to me, then maybe the NPR report would have floated past me that morning. But something about hearing that Africans are buried beneath a public street in a small, coastal New England town gave me a new context to reconsider what is obvious and how one might learn to live with it. I knew I had to go there to see the people, even if they were still tucked in tight, if I was ever going to start letting go of the expectation that I could someday feel less lonely in America.

The first time I drove the two hours north from Providence to Portsmouth I had no idea what I was going to do when I got there. It was a Sunday in late February, the day after a large snowfall had dumped about six inches of snow along New England's southern coast. By morning, the roads were no longer wet and the snow drifts at the side of the road glowed while ghostly wisps of fine powder swirled in the winnows of eighteen-wheelers trying to close the distance by Monday. From the interstate, I saw a sign for the Strawbery Banke Museum, which had been mentioned in the radio report, and I followed its direction.

The museum turned out to be a neighborhood of restored colonial houses at the edge of the Piscataqua River. The main entrance was closed, so I followed an elderly white couple into Stoodley's Tavern, which served as the museum ticket office on weekends. An older white woman with silver bobbed hair sat at a table covered with pamphlets advertising local tourist attractions. *Are you here for the tour?* she asked. I nodded yes. *Ten dollars.* Charles, our docent, chatted about the weather with the five of us who waited for the tour to begin: me, the senior couple who were from Kittery, Maine, and a very young, blond couple just recently moved to Vermont from Tahoe, Nevada.

We walked across the street into the original settlement founded in 1630, known as Puddle Dock. The Old Mainer wanted to know: *Where were the borders of the marsh before the houses were built? Where had the water been pushed back to?* He was wearing a cap that said *USS Indianapolis.* Charles asked him if he was on the ship during WWII and he said yes. Charles said, *Were you on it when it went down?* The Old Mainer told us that he had gone ashore at Pearl Harbor just before the ship had set sail for Guam. Charles enthusiastically told us the story of how the ship sank, as if its history illuminated an unseen aspect of the tour. On July 30, 1945, the ship, en route from Guam to the Gulf of Leyte, was torpedoed by the Japanese. More than nine hundred sailors were hurled into cold, choppy water. Although they radioed US forces for help as they went down, no one came for four days. By August 8, at the end of the rescue effort, only 317 men of the 1,196 originally on board had survived. The rest had been picked off by sharks or drowned.

After looking through a few of the houses in Puddle Dock, the Old Mainer, his wife, and I fell behind the guide and the young couple, who bragged about the beehive stove in an eighteenth-century farmhouse they were thinking of buying and restoring. They asked questions about the interior design of every home we toured. I took copious notes on Portsmouth's history and in this, felt my dour mood lightening. Details were comforting. Charles told us that Portsmouth was an Anglican, not Puritan, settlement and that amongst its original inhabitants were seventy-two Africans and eight Danes. Many of the wealthiest families in town made their fortunes in "the trade" first by shipping food, lumber, livestock, and other goods to British colonies in the West Indies and then by carrying captured Africans to the Caribbean, Virginia, and Portsmouth from the late seventeenth century through much of the eighteenth. Throughout the tour Charles occasionally used the word "servant" but never the word "slave."

In an alcove at the top of a staircase in a house built in 1790, the Old Mainer said to me, *I'd never live in one of these old houses. They're too cold.* There were two pictures on the mantel over the fireplace in the dining room. One called *Emblem of Africa* featured a black man walking with a feathered headdress next to a tiger in the background. The other picture, *Emblem of Europe,* featured a white woman with a globe at her feet holding a book and a horn of plenty filled with fruit and flowers at the crook of her arm.

When the young couple asked about role of the Native population in the development of Portsmouth, Charles explained that they were not a factor: *Most died out before the town became sizable, after catching diseases from their contact with the Europeans,* he said.

At the end of the tour, I returned to Stoodley's Tavern to ask for directions to the slave graves mentioned in the radio report. Charles told me, *You can't see anything. There's nothing there.* I thought he meant that the site had not been commemorated or officially rededicated, but his reaction made me wonder if there was even a historical marker indicating the graveyard's boundaries. The woman who had sold me a ticket said, *They've been re-interred.* I told them I still planned to go and asked if Chestnut Street was close, since Portsmouth's downtown area is quite small. *Or should I drive?* I said. She responded tersely, *It doesn't matter. It's just an intersection.*

•

It was sharply cold and the wind was picking up when I arrived at Chestnut Street near the corner of Court. Several restored colonials now serving as lawyers' and doctors' offices lined the south side. On the north side there was a beauty salon and a sign indicating a "Drug Free School Zone." Other than these buildings, it seemed that there *was* nothing to see. As I rounded the corner at Chestnut and State, I noticed a brass plaque affixed to the clapboards of a house: *In colonial Portsmouth, segregation applied in death as in life. City officials approved a plan in 1705 that set aside this city block for a "Negro Burial Ground." It was close to town but pushed to what was then its outer edge. By 1813, houses were built over the site.* I got back in my car to write notes about what I found. This is when I realized my car was probably sitting on top of people. I knew I should feel something about that, but all I felt was a familiar loneliness creeping in on me.

The trip to Portsmouth had not elicited much outrage in me, even after I discovered that one of the oldest known gravesites of blacks in New England was neither green nor sacred space. I accepted the reality that the historic colonial houses—now the business residences of attorneys, hairstylists, insurance agents, and doctors—were considered by most people to be more valuable than the bodies down below them. But while I had thought that my lack of feelings while standing on people would allow me to forget that I had been standing on people, it didn't. Still, I had no intuition about how these dead Africans might have felt about being paved over, no feelings of ancestral connection to those buried below, and I heard no discernible voices calling to me from the depths of that darkness. I wondered if the woman at the museum had been right. Maybe the corner *was* just an intersection.

The ambivalence the folks at the Strawbery Banke Museum expressed for those buried beneath Portsmouth's downtown was all the more surprising when I later learned that the first bodies exhumed from the African Burying Ground had been housed at the museum before they were transported to the temporary laboratory. I assumed that my own lack of feeling was due, in part, to the randomness with which I had selected Portsmouth as the place to try to make sense of the remains of slavery in America. I had no personal connection to New Hampshire, no familial bond to any of the people buried there, and I became certain that was the reason I couldn't feel anything while standing on those Africans. I thought maybe I needed to visit a slave gravesite more closely related to my life if I was going to experience some true cathexis.

So once back in Rhode Island, I went to a talk given by Theresa Guzmán Stokes at Newport's Redwood Library about that city's largest African burial ground, called God's Little Acre, a gravesite founded in 1747. For more than twenty years, without city support, she had been maintaining its grounds out of personal respect for those buried there, clearing away litter and weeds and eventually establishing a fund to protect it. She runs a website about the cemetery, and she and her husband Keith Stokes, Executive Director of the Newport County Chamber of Commerce, are writing a book on the subject.

While introducing his wife, Stokes assured the small audience, *We're not interested in slavery. It's emotional and it separates people.* But the absurdity of slavery means it is practically impossible for anyone to contain all of the contradictions that arise when speaking of it. So despite his promise seconds earlier to refrain from talk of slavery Stokes started by explaining how often the term "servant" is used as a euphemism for "slave" in New England and how there is a presumption that Africans here were somehow "smarter" and treated better than those in the South. *This misperception*, he pushed, *is because people don't want to remember the dehumanization.* Without hesitating he went on to say, *Slavery is violent, grotesque, vulgar, and we are all implicated in how it denigrates humanity.*

According to a series of articles by Paul Davis running that same week in the *Providence Journal*, Newport was a hugely significant port in the North Atlantic slave trade and that from 1725 to 1807 more than one thousand trips were made to Africa in which more than one hundred thousand men, women, and children were forced into slavery in the West Indies, Havana, and throughout the American colonies. Guzmán Stokes explained how African people built many of the prominent colonial houses throughout New England, including those in Newport, and while many of those buildings remain restored in one form or another, just a handful of graves of Africans who made this contribution to the town's development can be found.

On my way to God's Little Acre, I came upon the tiny Newport Historical Cemetery #9, which Guzmán Stokes had also mentioned during her talk, but I could not figure out which graves belonged to Africans and which belonged to whites. A white woman was taking pictures of stones, so I asked her if she knew. She pointed to two graves in the corner. *These over here,* she said and then explained she had looked for information on African graves on the web before she left her home in Seattle. The woman told me she was originally from Connecticut, but when she decided to marry an African

American man in the 1970s, her family disowned her. She had four children with him, none of whom ever met her parents. She had brought her youngest daughter back East to visit historical sites for a vacation and confessed that she was glad she no longer lived in New England. *I couldn't take all of this "in your face" history. Like Thames Street, the blue stones*—she said, referring to the pavers on a road that edges Newport's harbor—*Each one of those stones represents an African. Every stone was from the ballast of a slave ship and was carried by a slave as he or she debarked.* When I called the Newport Historical Society to confirm this, Reference Librarian and Genealogist Bert Lippincott III, CG, insisted that stones like that were used as ballast on all ships coming into Newport, not just slave ships. He added, *Many Newporters bankrolled ships in the trade, but Newport was not a major destination for slave ships.* When I mentioned the article in the *Providence Journal* that claimed most Africans in colonial Newport were slaves, he said, *Many were third-generation Americans. Most were skilled, literate, and worked as house servants.*

At God's Little Acre on the edge of Newport, three stones stand erect, three others appear jackknifed into the ground at a forty-five-degree angle. One lies level to the ground. Only these seven tombstones remain in the graveyard that commemorates the contributions of

Africans to the city's early history. While surrounded on three sides by larger, crowded cemeteries and an eight-foot wrought-iron fence facing Farewell Street, God's Little Acre is comparatively pastoral, and most of the grave markers are missing as a result of vandalism or landscaping contractors running tractor mowers though it. The inscriptions on those few slate stones still standing are fading due to the way weather and pollution wear on them. Many are now just barely legible.

A white woman with a backpack was taking pictures of the scant stones. She told me she teaches courses on American graveyards at a school in Connecticut. Pointing to one of the graves, she said, *He must have been loved by his "family"because stones were very expensive back then.* I wanted to say, *So were people.* And then I remembered reading an inventory from the estate of Joseph Sherburne whose house has been preserved at the Strawbery Banke Museum. The linens were listed to be worth forty dollars while the African woman who washed and pressed them had a line item value of fifty dollars.

My trip to Newport made me realize that I knew almost nothing about the lives of blacks in Portsmouth during slavery and I wondered if *that* was the reason I was so unmoved by my visit. So I drove back up to New

Hampshire to walk the Black Heritage Trail, put together by a retired schoolteacher and local historian, Valerie Cunningham, in order to learn about the experiences of Africans and African Americans in Portsmouth. Some of the sites on the Black Heritage Trail highlight historic accomplishments such as the New Hampshire Gazette Printing Office where Primus, a skilled slave, operated a printing press for fifty years; the Town Pump and Stocks where black leaders were elected in a ritual following loosely from the Ashanti festival tradition of Odwira; and St. John's Church, where the records indicate that Venus, most likely a poor but free black woman, received a gift of one dollar from the church in 1807 on Christmas Day.

I sat on a bench overlooking the Sarah Mildred Long Bridge, which crosses the Piscataqua River into Kittery, Maine, to where captive Africans would have first encountered Portsmouth, the wharf at what is now Prescott Park. The first known African captive arrived in Portsmouth around 1645 from Guinea, and slave ships started landing regularly as early as 1680 carrying small loads of mostly male children and adolescents. I tried to imagine what it felt like to come into this swiftly-moving river harbor after a long journey across the Atlantic in the cargo hold of a ship—after having been starved, beaten, shackled, and covered in the feculence of the living and dead. Did seeing for the first time the flat, tidy fronts of buildings outlining this colonial settlement make them feel hopeful? So many rectangles. How far away the rest of the world must have seemed.

I ended my walk at the Portsmouth Public Library, which held no significance on the trail, but, according to the first news story I heard about the burial ground, had in its collection a copy of the archaeologists' report on the burial site. When I asked a reference librarian if I could see it, she hesitated and wanted to know if I planned on making copies. I told her I was not sure if I wanted to make copies because I hadn't yet seen the report. She then consulted with the head reference librarian who told me that the burial site is a very sensitive issue for the city and that he needed to consult with the City Attorney's Office before releasing it. He took down my information—name, city of residence, and school affiliation—then asked me to wait while he placed the call.

The librarian was worried about how I might represent Portsmouth in a piece on the subject because he cared about the town. I liked the town, too. It is pretty, easy to navigate, and surprisingly friendly for New England. I felt guilty and ashamed about my affinity for the town because at the time I could not muster more than a diffuse intellectual identification with the people who were buried just a few streets over.

Before copying the report, I remembered how easy it was for me to ignore what was already obvious, so I wrote down some details to remind myself of what I shouldn't forget: people were carried like chattel on ships to America; they were sold to other people; they were stripped of their names, spiritual practices, and culture; they worked their entire lives without just compensation; they were beaten into submission and terrorized or killed if they chose not to submit; when they died they were buried in the ground at the far edge of town; and as the town grew, roads and houses were built on top of them as if they had never existed.

I spent the long summer with my friends at the beach, drinking Bloody Marys and eating lobster rolls on the open-air deck of a clam shack in Galilee, Rhode Island, while the Block Island Ferry, serried with tourists, made its lethargic heave past the docked commercial fishing boats. Once school started, I turned my attention back to the spiritless tedium of lesson planning and grading papers. In all that time I did not once touch the archaeologists' report.

I could make something up about why I let the report sit in a manila folder on my desk for nine months without ever once attempting to read it—something about wanting to let the dead rest or about how loneliness swells and recedes—but I won't. The reason is not clear to me even now. What I do know is that holding the copy I had made of the report near the Xerox machine by the dimly lit front door of the Portsmouth Public Library that previous spring made me feel more than I had felt during any of my gravesite visits, like a balloon in my chest was expanding and taking up all the space I normally used to breathe.

Intense discomfort, I had thought. *Maybe that's enough.*

But by January I was driving back up to Portsmouth, irritated with myself for not reading the copy of the report I had already made but even more irritated with myself for not being able to let it go unread. The once tattered and gloomy public library had moved to a brilliant new building a few streets over, and as I walked around the landscapers installing the brick steps, I caught the sign on the door that said, *Welcome to Your New Library.* In the breezeway, three junior high school girls gathered around a computer terminal and giggled. A woman in a purple cardigan greeted me from behind the circulation desk with a smile and thin wave. Seduced by all of it, I thought, *I love my new library.*

When I asked the reference librarian about the

report, he told me it was now shelved in the local history section in the regular stacks. I thought, *Now it's all out in the open. Now there's nothing to hide.* I grabbed it off the wall, took a seat at one of the new blond reading tables and thumbed through it lightly as if it were a mere tabloid magazine. I took notes from the acknowledgments, introduction, and background chapters, but when I got to the section describing the removal of the coffins—those same pages I had copied nearly a year before—a shrill noise came up from the back of my throat at the pitch of a full tea kettle in a rolling-boil whistle. I cleared my throat and went back to reading, but my din started again. It was sharp enough for anyone to hear, so I decided I had better leave—but not before making a fresh copy of the report to take with me.

When a story is unpleasant, it is hard to focus on details that allow you to put yourself in the subject's place because the pain of distortion starts to feel familiar. Paying attention often requires some sort of empathy for the subject, or at the very least, for the speaker. But empathy, these days, is hard to come by. Maybe this is because everyone is having such a hard time being understood themselves. Or because empathy requires us to dig way down into the murk, deeper than our own feelings go, to a place where the boundaries between our experience and everyone else's no longer exist.

Archaeologists removed the remains of thirteen people from beneath the intersection of Chestnut and Court Streets with the help of some machinery, but they did most of the digging by hand. Once in the laboratory, they used potter's tools and paintbrushes to remove excess soil from the bones and teeth. The exact dates associated with each burial remain unknown, but it is assumed that all were interred during the eighteenth century. Four males and one female could be identified by sex, but they found it impossible to determine the sex of the other eight, though most were believed to be in early adulthood, between the ages of twenty-one and forty years. Heads of the deceased generally faced west, suggesting a burial in the Christian tradition. In no cases were all the bones of an individual represented, perhaps due to the commingling of remains during previous installations of gas and sewer lines, the stacking of coffins, or a high water table in the soil. Thus no cause of death could be determined for any of those recovered. Archaeologists noted, however, that the lack of visible traumatic defects, cut marks, fresh or healed fractures does not rule out the presence of trauma. The teeth of each person, which in several cases constituted the entirety of the remains, appeared to be better preserved than their bones, which were found wet, free of flesh, colored gray or black and, in the case of long bones, often missing the ends.

Pieces of the skull, portions of the upper and lower limbs, shoulder girdle, ribs, spine, and pelvis of a male person between the ages of twenty-one and thirty years represent Burial 1. An excavator operator noticed his leg bones sticking out from the bottom of his coffin, which was made of white pine and was hexagonal in shape. All of his mandibular and some of his maxillary teeth were present, but like most of those recovered at the site, his teeth exhibit traces of enamel hypoplasia, a sign of previous infection or nutritional stress. His bones revealed a calcified blood vessel in his right lower leg and prolonged shin splints. A pumpkin seed of unexplained significance was found in his coffin as well as a metal object, probably a shroud pin, suggesting he was naked at burial.

In Burial 2, the remains of another male person between twenty-one and twenty-six years of age were found in good condition despite the fact that part of his skull had been unintentionally crushed by the excavator, leaving only his mandible and several teeth. A gas line running through the foot portion of his coffin meant that many bones in his right foot also were missing. His body was slumped to the left side, probably due to his coffin being tipped during burial, and his hipbone was broken in several places. His right hand lay over his thigh. Further analysis of his bones showed signs of repetitive forearm rotation and possible inflammation of the right leg, presumably from heavy shoveling, lifting, or other strenuous work. Salt, either used as a preservative before burial or for some other ritual, and a single tooth of unknown origin found between his knees, further distinguished his remains.

Burial 3 contained the remains of a person of indeterminate sex, thought to be approximately thirty to fifty years of age with the head facing east, perhaps toward Mecca. Archaeologists recovered only extremely fragile fragments of the cranium and major long bones. The part of the mandible that was still intact suggests participation in a West African puberty ritual as there is a long-healed-over gap where lower and lateral incisors would have been. Stains in the soil represented most of the coffin wood. Only thirty teeth, small fragments of bone, some wood and coffin nails accounted for the person of twenty-one to forty years of age in Burial 4. Those remains were extremely damaged by erosion and the unintentional intrusion of the excavator.

Pipe laid around 1900 across the bottom of the coffin of the male person aged twenty-one to forty in Burial 5 eventually disintegrated his lower extremities. Shovel marks on the coffin base indicate where a crew member either hit his coffin accidentally or attempted to cut through it.

The head of the female person in Burial 6 was located under the sidewalk, which had to be caved in to allow for her removal. Only the upper portion of her coffin was found intact. Her lower legs, cut off where they intersected with a utility trench and a ceramic sewage pipe installed around 1900, revealed evidence of a bone infection and severe inflammation of the shins. Her left arm appeared to be laid across her torso, and her cranium, now missing the face, pointed to the right side of the coffin. Her upper central incisors were shaved, possibly according to a West African cultural tradition, and represent the earliest documented case of such dental modification in North America.

The person in Burial 7 was a child between the ages of seven and twelve, of unknown sex, whose remains were damaged by heavy rain and a redirected sewer line that flooded the graveshaft during excavation. Decades of a sewer pipe lying across the child's midsection also contributed to this poor state, despite the fact that the coffin was found to be in relatively good condition. Directly beneath that body were the remains of a male person between twenty-one and forty years of age in Burial 12 whose bones were very soft due also to the high water table of the soil. At present, it is impossible to tell if these two people were buried at the same time or possibly even generations apart. The coffinless remains of persons in Burials 2B, 3B, 4B, 5B, and 7B were discovered beneath the sidewalk. Dental fragments and hand bones from a person not presently attributed to Burial 2 but found nearby are all that exists of the person in Burial 2B. Twelve teeth represent the person in Burial 3B. One tooth each indicates persons in Burials 4B and 5B, and a femur shaft fragment resting atop the child's coffin in Burial 7 is all that was found of the person in Burial 7B.

The boundaries of Portsmouth's African Burying Ground are still a mystery, as they have been for more than one hundred years, but plans to build a formal memorial are underway. Public discussions led by the state's archaeologists have asked city residents to consider whether a part of either street should be closed to vehicular traffic. Some Portsmouth residents have submitted samples of their DNA to see if they are in any way related to those people whose remains, now stored in Ethafoam, 0.002 mil polybags, and acid-free archival storage boxes in a municipally provided laboratory space, await reinterment.

Because I worried that I would lose track of the

archaeologists' report amongst the bills, magazines, and student papers that littered my desk, for many months I kept it beside my bed, on the floor beneath my nightstand. Each morning the radio woke me with news of the war, a pop star's addiction, dismal predictions for the American economy. Later, I put the report in my backpack, its pages flat against my spine. At some point, I am not sure when, I grew accustomed to its weight and stopped noticing I was carrying it around.

Chicago Radio

IN 2005 MORE THAN a million black people lived in Chicago, Illinois, making it a good place to win friends and stop being a stranger.

Other predominantly black cities like St. Louis, Missouri, and Detroit, Michigan, experienced frequent sightings of UFOs.

●

Listening to music underwater affects one's hearing in curious ways. No visible change can be seen in the shape of the eardrum, but many report being able to hear whispers from people they have never met for days after coming to the surface. Investigations into this phenomenon have been labeled crackpot science and hoodoo though amongst astrologers and criminologists interest grows.

•

CALLER: My name is Mimi, and I would like to dedicate a song for my dad.

DJ: Go ahead.

CALLER: Just start talking?

DJ: Just start talking.

CALLER: His name is Earl. The last time I saw him he was working as an electrician for Delta Airlines at O'Hare in 1995.

Dad, you can come home now, and please don't worry too much about the past. This song has no words because I don't want to make any more promises.

I still love you.

•

Geography and racial inequality work against even the most nutritionally conscious moms.

A study of 266 black women in Detroit found that those who shopped in supermarkets ate more servings of fruits and vegetables per day than those who shopped at independent neighborhood grocery stores.

One area of Detroit that was 97% African American had no chain supermarkets and twelve independent grocery stores.

A nearby mixed-race area had ten independent groceries and seven chain supermarkets.

•

New data about the connections between nutrition and violence is changing the way people think about prison. Oxford University scientist Bernard Gesch tracked 231 maximum-security inmates for twelve months, recording violent or antisocial incidents. He gave one group a vitamin supplement, while a control group got a placebo. Over the next several months he saw a 35% drop in fighting amongst the group receiving vitamin supplements.[1]

•

CALLER: I would like you to play a song for my fiancé.
           I don't know which one, can you pick it?

DJ: Sure thing. Hey, how did he propose?

CALLER: It was pretty plain.

DJ: Oh yeah? What did he do?

CALLER: He said, *I want you to be my wife. Do you want
           to be my wife?*

DJ: That doesn't sound plain to me. When are
           you getting married?

CALLER: We don't know. He's overseas right now.

DJ: Fighting?

CALLER: Yeah.

•

Rather than suffer the indignities of slavery, hundreds
of thousands of Africans chose to drown while crossing

the Atlantic. Some DJs claim no one drowned at all and those who leapt from deck landed below the ocean on a subcontinent called Drexciya.[2]

It can be hard to get a message through when people are underwater.

•

Police officer Martin Farr described the evacuation of a Chicago public high school after the storm passed:

A woman, she was about the age of my mother, maybe fifty years or so, was standing at a podium in front of a large classroom. She spoke to her students in a stern tone of voice about personal responsibility. When I turned around to note their reaction, I realized the back half of the building had been blown away by the storm. Torn strips of corrugated steel hung over a gaping hole in which oily, brown water was rushing in. Soon it was up to our chests. The teacher seemed unmoved by the flood, but she was overcome with disappointment in her students' inability to call out their presence at attendance.

•

A glowing red object flew over a residential area of New Haven, Connecticut, in November 1953, causing lights on both sides of the object's path to dim and then come back on when it went out of sight. This signified the beginning of an increase in New Haven's black population.

In 1950, African Americans comprised only 12.25% of New Haven's population. By 2000, New Haven was 43.5% White and 37.4% African American.[3]

•

A plane filled with prisoners being transported to a federal facility in Wyoming took off from Chicago's O'Hare airport in April. Ascending into low clouds over Lake Michigan, it disappeared from radar. The plane showed up several hours later near the Florida Keys, heading toward a tropical storm gathering force off the western coast of Cuba. For about thirty minutes Miami controllers tried to reestablish radio contact. When the plane vanished for the final time, all the controllers involved in the search fell asleep and were unable to be wakened for one hour.

•

DJ: Who am I talking to?

CALLER: This is James.

DJ: James, what can I do for you tonight?

CALLER: Could you play a song for my baby's mother? We're not getting along too good, and I just want her to know that I love her.

DJ: What's going on?

CALLER: Well, ever since our daughter was born she has been afraid to leave her with me because I am visually impaired.

DJ: Did she know you were visually impaired when you, you know, conceived your daughter?

CALLER: Yes.

DJ: And now she has an issue with that?

CALLER: Yes, well—

DJ: Do you think that she really has an issue with that or is she mad about something else?

CALLER: Uh—

DJ: Is there anything else that might be worrying her?

CALLER: I just want her to know that I plan on being a really good dad and that I love her, I love them both a lot.

DJ: I'm sorry you are having such a hard time, James, and I hope the two of you can work it out.

CALLER: Can you play a song for me?

DJ: Not right now.

●

This account comes from a former member of the Chicago Police Department, now working as a security guard for a local supermarket chain.

A soldier recently returned from the war was teaching his eight-year-old brother combat techniques for a shoreline invasion. They dug a trench wide enough to hold them both and then enacted the kind of gestures they would perform in response to a heavy artillery attack. The younger brother grew bored with the exercise and pleaded to go home. The older brother, overcome with thoughts of war, sat down for a moment to collect himself. A sudden surge from the lake surprised him. He was knocked unconscious by the force of the wave and dragged under as his younger brother watched from the hill.

When the younger brother finally made his way home, he was unable to speak. I was called in to raise the elder brother from the dead so that the younger one might convey his regret in being unable to save him. We went back to the beach. Because the surf was still choppy from the recent storm, it was not difficult to conjure the spirit of the soldier. His face looked badly scratched and bruised. When he tried to talk, only sand and water came out of his mouth. The younger brother made his apology. The soldier accepted this apology begrudgingly because things had not turned out how he thought they would. He extended his hand to his young brother. That contact left a permanent scar on the boy's hand, a smooth, white patch in the shape of a "Y" that would itch whenever the boy became frightened.

•

For several summers in a cemetery on the city's South Side a man grew turnips and mustard greens, spinach, callaloo, and rapini on the plot that would become his grave. Each crop had grown quite large. He claimed he fed himself for the entire winter on what he raised on his narrow field, but this year someone stole his harvest.

A police officer doubted they would find the perpetrator. The other officer handed the man a bag of groceries he had picked up for his family just before the call. Inside the bag there were canned peas and carrots, green beans, corn, and white potatoes.

•

DJ: Go ahead with your long-distance dedication.

CALLER: This song is for my grandmother, who taught me how to use coupons to shop around to get the best prices on groceries. She bought a green Pinto in 1970, and we used to go everywhere together.

DJ: You guys used to go out on little adventures, huh? Where did she take you?

CALLER: Well, we would start out at Food Town in Quakertown, Pennsylvania, where we bought evaporated milk, biscuit mix, and sardines.

And then we would head to Zeller's in Windsor, Ontario, where we bought canned Jamaican akee fruit for her next-door neighbors, Mr. and Mrs. MacDonald, who said it tasted like scrambled eggs.

At Farmer Jack's in Troy, Michigan, we stocked up on dried pinto beans, shredded coconut, long-grain white rice and canned whole tomatoes.

At Cub Foods in Chicago we carried out cases of canned corn and green beans along with gallon jugs of blended scotch whiskey and gin.

She once filled an entire suitcase with dry ice and shrimp fresh off the boat in New Orleans, Louisiana before driving us back home to Jamaica, Queens, in New York.

DJ: And where is your grandmother now?

CALLER: Right here beside me waiting for her song.

Notes

1. Broadcast on CBS, affiliated radio station WBZ-AM 1030 (Boston, MA) on April 28, 2004.

2. James Stinson founded the techno group Drexciya in Detroit in 1994. He died suddenly in 2002 at the age of thirty-two.

3. According to the 2000 census.

Cleveland

THE DOCUMENTARY WAS A RUSE I devised in order
to spend intimate time with Adrienne Kennedy, the
esteemed experimental playwright. I believed talking
with her would give me insight into why I suffered so
much in my own creative life. After she turned me down
twice, a friend who took two of her classes at Harvard
asked her to meet me at Café Algiers for a brief interview as a personal favor to him. She agreed as long as I
promised not to use a recording device.

Kennedy was surprised to find me still waiting for
her when she arrived over an hour late. Perhaps she
already knew that I was less interested in her life than

in my interpretation of it. She did not respond when I introduced myself, and she would not shake my hand before sitting down. Staring out the window at the parking lot, she seemed to be startled by a seagull that landed on the ledge. Gesturing toward the bird she said, *No one can destroy anyone else.* Then she lifted her cup to her lips, her hand shaking. As she set it down, coffee splashed across the saucer.

Kennedy asked if we could speak off the record before the interview. I put down my pen. She whispered she had been delayed because she had hurt someone. Her voice cracked at the word "hurt."

A collision. Not for vengeance for strife or justice, she murmured. A wave of her hand indicated that was all she wanted to say about it. She told me I should begin with my questions as she had only few more minutes to spend with me.

I started with what I thought would be an easy-to-answer question about Chekhov—if she thought her voice was in any way related to his. Kennedy said she felt like Chekhov had asked her the same thing while she was reading a new translation of *The Cherry Orchard* during the fall of 2008, at the beginning of the global market upheaval. She said Chekhov would have found my preoccupation with voice amusing, how I thought I could hear what had gotten away from me.

I wanted to tell her that once when reading a new translation of Chekhov's works I also heard him whispering that all previous versions had captured what he meant to say only partly right. Then I thought that would be revealing too much about my desire to insert myself into her experience.

I inquired about her feelings about being a playwright, given her high standing in the theatre. She turned her face toward the window and said crisply, *No one is waiting for me.*

When I pressed her to explain what she meant, she asked me about my plans for children. I told her my husband had recently left me for a woman he was having a child with and my ambivalence about motherhood came out of my fear that I would not know how to parent a child of mixed race. When I mentioned her children were often subjects in her plays, she declined to speak of them at all. After that, she excused herself.

I had not given Kennedy an honest answer as to why I did not want children, but the truth was something I found so unremarkable I dared not repeat it. I feared having a child who was like me would amplify my sense of failure, causing me to feel resentment all the time. I could hold my feelings in, suppressing rage, which might then manifest as depression, bitterness, or a lack of ambition. If I could not control my anger, there might be long-term consequences. Yelling at a child affects their heart. A rise in adrenaline and cortisol is a natural response to danger, but if experienced frequently, such attacks may result in heart disease.

I was not recovering well from the disappointment of my failed marriage. My ex-husband had not been honest about wanting to have a child, and he had resented me for not coaxing him into fatherhood.

It made me angry to think of how I could not let go of my desire to touch him. Sharp and final as our separation had been, our coming together had been more impacting. When we met, he was acting in one of my plays. The euphoria I experienced in the early days of our relationship inspired me to rewrite the ending just before we opened for previews. Perhaps because of this or another failure in foresight on my part, the play turned out to be a flop.

A few weeks later *The New York Times* reported that so many teachers had been laid off in Cleveland since the beginning of the recession that public school classrooms were now expected to have more than forty students. One teacher noted that tenure and nine years of experience in the classroom did not safeguard her from unemployment. She thought it seemed ironic that with all the talk about the importance of education during downtimes, teachers were often the first civic employees to be let go.

Something about this story caught my interest, so I drove to Ohio to pursue more research. I arrived in town near the end of the trial of the notorious serial killer Anthony Sowell, who would be sentenced to death for killing and disposing of at least eleven women in his home on Imperial Avenue. Body parts had been wrapped in sheets and black plastic bags and left strewn throughout his house. Most of his victims were reported as missing, but because they had criminal records as prostitutes and drug addicts, police did not investigate their disappearances.

As I passed the Cleveland Public Library, I noted the Adrienne Kennedy Society was holding a reading of *The Ohio State Murders,* one of her plays. When I went to buy a ticket for the event, I was told it had been cancelled due to the fear that the content of the play would provoke the audience to violence.

The next day, I read in *The Plain Dealer* that Kennedy had planned to make a surprise appearance at the reading. She found out it had been called off only when she arrived to find the doors locked.

During the ride down I heard a public radio show about underappreciated American writers, and it was reported that Kennedy had taken temporary residence in a suburb of Cleveland for the summer in order to research a new play she was writing about post-traumatic stress disorder.

In the days after hearing the broadcast I thought about her so hard I imagined I could see the words she was putting down as she composed her next work. One evening after drinking half a bottle of wine, my thoughts made me feel as if I was close enough to her to read what she was writing. It was almost as if I was standing in her study, looking over her shoulder. Her piece said something about how being excluded felt like the rending of skin. She wrote: "Though there could be no visible scar from this disappointment, a sense of injury from being left out changed the way I saw myself. I was never whole after that."

During my visit to Ohio, two incidents moved me in a way I could not shake. The first was an encounter with a woman who oversaw the entrance to the Cleveland Botanical Garden. I met her when I attended a cocktail and sustainable foods party at the end of the summer. I was hoping to meet a man I liked there and was feeling self-conscious about my hair when another woman handed me a tube of lotion. It had a calming affect on my curls, and smoothing them made me feel less artsy, more predictable-looking, at least. We talked about the murders for which Sowell had just been convicted. *Someone should have been looking for them,* she said.

What struck me about our conversation was the tone in her voice, which evidenced a deep empathy for women. She admitted to knowing little about the neighborhood in which the bodies had been found, but since their discovery, she had gone out of her way to drive by there on her way to work. She did this exercise once a week, in order to force herself to think about those whose absences had not been counted.

Last month she was involved in an accident with a hit-and-run driver in front of Sowell's residence. Though the house had been razed and in its place grew a fresh field of native plants, the woman could not bear to wait in her dented car that had stalled out in front of the lot. Thankfully, a neighbor on the corner who called a tow service let her sit and wait for their arrival on his porch.

The second incident occurred at one of Kennedy's plays, which dramatized her life as a playwright. On stage an actor playing Kennedy as a middle-aged woman took notes on the agonies of Kennedy's life as a younger person, who was played by the ingénue. From where I sat in the audience, I could see the real Kennedy seated at the back of the house. She had a notebook opened in her lap, though she wasn't writing anything down.

At intermission, I followed her to the restroom. She did not seem to recognize me from our previous meeting at the diner, but I had no expectation that she would.

At the signal to return to our seats, I watched Kennedy head toward the lobby instead of back into the theatre. I followed her out into the street where she continued, at somewhat of a leisurely pace, up the avenue, past a number of closed cafés and over-lit drugstores through a set of gray doors that opened up to the dark lobby of a hotel. An oversized black crystal chandelier hanging in the center of the lobby was not lit. Kennedy went up to the front desk where she was greeted by name and given a keycard. I thought about following her into the elevator, but I felt too conspicuous and chose to sit on one of the cognac leather chairs in the corridor leading to the hotel's library. I picked up a copy of that day's *Plain Dealer* where I learned Kennedy had also attended the cocktail party at the Botanical Garden.

•

A picture describing the event showed her standing in the Restorative Garden shaking hands with the director of the board. I had spent most of the evening in that same part of the park, sipping wine in the outdoor classroom adjacent to the pool garden. How had I missed her?

My intense interest in Kennedy was rooted in a fundamental insecurity I couldn't overcome. I became aware of the problem when I started reading her plays during my junior year of college. There I had suffered from social isolation due to my anxiety about my racial identity, which was black, though seldom recognized as such due to my fair skin. Part of the confusion about who I was had to do with the way I presented myself. I have always been seasons behind with regards to styles in fashion and hair, in part due to the fact that I am naturally slow to notice trends. Other reasons why I have failed to be recognized as myself are beyond my understanding, but I am certain they have contributed to my lack of success as an artist.

There have been times when I felt anger for failing to reap rewards commensurate with the energy I put forth in my creative work and relationships. There are times when I got so frustrated about the ways individuals failed to see me that I wanted to kick them to ensure they would have strong feelings for me. I try to channel that rage into my work. Sometimes I succeed. Other times, I need to leave a room as quickly as possible to make sure no one gets hurt because I believe that, when an expression of will includes brutality of the physical sort, the desire to explain the violation can never redress the wound. Violence fails to make a point beyond demonstrating a lack of control. Bluntness works better to emphasize misperception, even though it is often imprecise. Eventually the question arises as to whether or not suffering is inevitable. Any answer given can make sense at the time.

Kennedy's play about PTSD featured a black woman searching for the source of her anger in her personal and political history. It was lauded by the critics but failed to win an audience. One review cited the age of the main character as a possible reason for the less than full house. She was no longer young and yet not old enough to sentimentalize, thus the dialogue demanded the audience pay attention to contradictions between what the character said and did. This attention to psychology made the play, in the opinion of the critic, "complicated."

•

I spent much of the next year writing my play about Cleveland, but all my characters seemed exaggerated no matter how much they had been informed by research. Just as I was on the verge of giving up, I got a call from a local blogger who had heard about the project. She wanted to interview me though I feared I had little to share. My efforts to say something important about missing women felt incomplete.

The interview took place over the phone and lasted two hours. While discussing some of the incidents that led to my research, I confessed that any interest in my work made me anxious, and I had a tendency to accentuate the least important details.

The young woman never posted her blog entry. Apparently when she attempted to transcribe the conversation, she discovered the recording was full of dropouts. My sentences seldom finished and kept fading into whisper.

Manhattanville, Part One

1.

The first time I was mistaken for my son's nanny, I did not criticize the offending woman's lack of imagination out loud. We had stopped in the market on the way home from his doctor's office so I could get a sandwich. My son, only six weeks old at the time, relaxed facing forward on my chest, his eyes focused on the cool white of refrigerated shelves. When the woman said to me, *Does his mother know you kiss him like that?* the only retort I could think of was, *I am his mother.*

My husband is Jewish. I am African American. According to conservative social standards, our son does not qualify as either. We suspected this would be the case. After he was born, my hair grew straighter than it had ever been. The implications of this change, if I paid attention, would make anyone concerned with authenticity anxious.

It is fair to acknowledge that my personal choices had made it such that I could fail to prove myself truly black to any critic embracing orthodoxy. Though once I was busy caring for my son, my preoccupations with race shifted away from legitimating my own identity to seeking out a community that would acknowledge his.

I believed that by allowing myself to assume his two-ness, I might acquire greater sensitivity to his experience. But my efforts at empathy were frustrated by the fact that my son has his father's complexion and is often presumed to be only white.

We lived in Manhattanville, a historically diverse neighborhood bordering the community of Morningside Heights, where a prominent university anchors a burgeoning middle class. My husband attended the university for graduate school, and I spent a year there doing research while completing my own graduate degrees. We both enjoyed having access to its library and cultural events, though I did not look forward to the fall arrival of students who would insist through their late-night displays of drunkenness and sexual discovery that our neighborhood belongs to them.

•

For most of the nineteenth century, Manhattanville was home to several prominent religious, educational, and social institutions invested in elevating the poorest members of the city into better circumstances. In 1822, the Hebrew Benevolent and Orphan Asylum was established at Amsterdam and 136th Street. Another Jewish charity, The Montefiore Home for Chronic Invalids provided care for individuals who could not get treatment elsewhere. An orphanage called The Sheltering Arms received poor children, regardless of creed or nationality, who had been temporarily surrendered by their parents. The Manhattanville Nursery on Old Broadway and 131 Street, established in 1916, served as a day and night shelter, playground, and kindergarten. Its founders believed the family to be "the strategic point of economic efficiency."

After the university decided to increase in size by building a campus in our part of the city, they purchased dozens of buildings, and then exerted minimal effort in maintaining them. This process of neglect began years before I met my husband or considered having a child with him. In spite of our relative newness to the neighborhood, something about the university's expansion felt invasive once the demolition began. All day we watched red and yellow cranes bob and pivot against a gray sky.

•

When our son was two, my husband took him to Old Broadway Synagogue, the oldest temple in Harlem, on Yom Kippur. Black men and white men davening together inspired him to commence his own rocking rhythm though he was not yet old enough for words.

•

Some of the first words my son favored were *viaduct, escalator, taxi,* and *bodega,* all of which were appropriate given that our apartment faced two decorative iron train bridges at the southwestern border of Harlem, the spot where green taxis abound and yellow taxis make U-turns to retreat downtown.

The location of our apartment also allowed us to witness traffic patterns of the trains, buses, cars, helicopters, and planes. From our bedroom window we could also see down 125th Street to where passengers waited on the station's trestle. We watched jets making their final descent to LaGuardia Airport. Our grocery store faced the Hudson River, and my son first learned about construction by studying the George Washington Bridge. During our walks through Riverside Park, he would often notice the sound of helicopters tracking the traffic along the West Side Highway long before they came into view. Then he would beg of the sky, *More. More. More.*

When our son was just walking, we used to take him to a park across the street from Grant's Tomb. Red double-decker tour buses stopped here so tourists could take pictures and buy bottles of water. One day near the end of the summer, our son was playing in a fountain when he noticed a curly-headed blond girl in a bright green swimsuit. She appeared to be about three. The girl waved to get his attention, but each time he got close he turned bashful and ran back to me. Her mother and father sat across from us, cooing over their newborn shaded by the stroller. The father was a white man with reddish brown hair, and her mother was brown-skinned like me. When we rolled the stroller out of the park, on instinct my son and I waved good-bye, though none of us had actually spoken. Smiling, they waved back to us.

•

Two high-rise public housing facilities in Manhattanville, one on the north side of 125th Street and one on the south have a history of tension between residents. The Manhattanville Houses and Grant Houses were designed as mixed-race units in the late 1950s. At the time of construction, these buildings held the distinction of being the city's tallest developments. Of the first five families to move there, two were white, two were black, and one was Puerto Rican.

On the tenth anniversary of 9/11, a Sunday morning in early September, we heard women shrieking and sobbing at dawn outside the entrance to the Grant Houses on Broadway. Later when I walked by, no one at any of the bodegas seemed to know what had happened beyond a bad fight during the night. The next day I saw a report on the local television news about the murder of one of the top high-school point guards in the country, possibly in retaliation for a scuffle her brother was rumored to have been involved in at the nearby C-Town grocery store on 125th Street. Eighteen-year-old Tayshana Murphy, a senior at Murry Bergtraum High School for Business Careers, was shot three times as she pleaded for her life. Reporters speculated that her death might have been provoked by a long-standing series of conflicts between youth in the two housing developments.

About a week before the shooting of the young woman, my husband had heard gunshots in the middle of the night. He grabbed our son from his crib, and we huddled in the hallway until police arrived and dispersed the brawling crowd in the streets. The next morning, we hurried to work and school just as we did every day.

•

The director of our son's daycare understood the importance of art in the formation of children's imagination and that was one of the primary reasons we enrolled him in the program. The other reason we chose the school had to do with the fact that three of the children in his class of ten had black mothers and Jewish fathers. With thirty percent of the room sharing our son's demographic we figured the questions about his identity could be tabled until the children learned to converse.

One day my son's teacher mentioned he had been walking around the classroom announcing he was "black and Jewish." She thought it was especially funny because she assumed I was *Latin or something like that.*

I told her I was African American. She pushed back, saying, *But you're mixed, right?* That's when I went into the rich history of my family: my mother from Queens and her parents from Harlem and the Bronx, my dad's people from Alabama and Tennessee, the Great Migration, the promise of the five-dollar day working at the Ford plants in Detroit during the war, the riots, and finally the 1970s, when I was most certainly black enough to not be considered anything else.

•

One afternoon at the daycare I was complaining with another mother, who was white, about how hard it was to get our boys to leave at the end of the day. We were in the process of coaxing our sons to set off for home when a woman who looked a lot like me came into the building to drop off an application. The boys squealed as they ran up and down the hall. When the visitor asked the other mother if the boys were twins, the other mother said, *One of them is mine, and one is hers.* The woman looked as if a terrible mistake had been made, and she crossed quickly in front of the children to exit.

•

I was standing outside the hardware store with my son when an older, white man approached me to say my boy looked just like me. I said he also favors his father, to which he responded, *Don't ever tell him that. He'll sell you off in an instant.* Then he looked at my son and said, *He looks just like you. Trust me. You don't want the father thinking anything else.* As my husband exited the store, a bag of mousetraps in hand, the man said, *This is the father?* and then hurried to confirm his point. *Don't let him sell you.*

•

Though I tried to get out of jury duty by boasting that my brother-in-law worked for the Department of Justice, I was assigned to be a juror in a criminal trial. The case turned out to be one of those specious "stop and frisk" ones, where the cops did not need to prove just cause in stopping the defendant and searching his car. He was arrested for criminal possession of a knife. The case was complicated by the fact that all of the witnesses appeared to have forgotten what happened on the night of the arrest. A lapse in memory was also apparent in the testimony of the arresting officers, who were no longer on good terms with each other.

Just prior to the trial, a fifteen-year-old boy from the Grant Houses had been slashed three times in the face. He survived the assault but refused to identify his attacker. Even though more than thirty kids saw the fight that led to the incident no one came forward as a witness.

•

My husband and I were at a baseball game when he received a text message from the university's department of public safety, explaining that three men had been shot in a car just a few blocks from our apartment. The men had been murdered in early evening, in broad daylight. When I dropped my son off at daycare the next morning, this was on everyone's mind but no one mentioned it. We just looked at each other, sighed, and shook our heads. It was rumored that the dead men had all been drug dealers, and conflicting reports described them as either thieves known for stealing from other dealers, or snitches. Each of their mothers claimed they were loving, loyal sons. All we knew for certain was that the men who had died were very young.

We walked home from a restaurant in early evening. When we passed the street where they had been killed, signs affixed to the parking meter read: *You don't / have to reveal / your identity / to help solve / violent crime.*

•

Often my son would not sit in the buggy when I picked him up from daycare, so as a compromise, I would let him walk to the corner. After that he would be secured in his stroller when we crossed Broadway during rush-hour traffic. When we arrived at the curb, he might buck and cry to get out, but that day I kept him harnessed in until we reached our stoop. We learned in the weeks that followed that the killer discarded his shirt in the trash bin precisely at the spot where daily I argued with my son to stay put. We might have passed him immediately following the shooting, though when I saw the picture of him from the security camera in the newspaper, I did not recognize his face.

In Search of the Face

A WOMAN I THOUGHT was a friend kept calling me impeccable. At first I mistook the word for a compliment. Eventually I realized her observation was cruel scrutiny, so I set out to see myself from every angle. This is how I discovered I am spherical, a ball bouncing over words illustrating a song that goes like this:

Yes! Yes! Yes!

•

I am thirteen. My neighbor, Mrs. Minetti, calls my mother and asks her to send me over to help with a few chores around the house.

Her son is dead.

She has a daughter living in West Virginia who will not speak to her.

She calls me over because I am about the same age her daughter was the first time she ran away.

Mrs. Minetti tells me how kids ruin even a very good marriage and how much a mother can love a daughter even if the daughter turns out to be a little whore.

Then she pays me five dollars and sends me home.

•

Pictures in the bookstore of elderly seniors having sex get me aroused.

I am not embarrassed admitting a preference for loose skin.

•

My friend and I sit at a café to catch up on the past year. Since I've last seen her, she has lost her husband and a kidney. I have gotten a new pair of glasses.

After a couple of cups of extra-sweet tea, we each confess how it is that we kill love.

I learned my technique from a short story, you know
how it goes—

I take love down into the basement, get it drunk on cheap
sherry. Once it's asleep, I brick up the door to the cellar.

My friend kills love by putting it into a lobster cage,
then rowing out to the middle of the ocean. When she
drops the cage into cold waters, she says,

See!?

•

A friend of a friend of mine thought he fell in love with
me. He was getting over an addiction to sugar, and I can
be terribly sweet.

Anyway, in the meantime.

A new woman came to town who looked just like me,
except for the fact that she was the daughter of a
famous comedian. One day I found her and my friend's
friend having sex in the faculty lounge.

They did a pretty good job.

•

I am on my way to Boston. A girl on the bus singing in Spanish has the worst voice I've ever heard.

I write down reasons why I probably love you and hate myself for falling for any song no matter how awful it sounds.

•

a head
a face
a ball
a bounce

a joke
a dress
a wish
a wall

a wrong
a game
a fall
a sea

a dish
a song
a bus
a tree

•

The composer gave a lecture on his new opera.

We had arranged for a special dinner in his honor, but he was otherwise committed to spending the evening with friends, he said.

I conveyed his regrets, called him a cab, then walked the long way home past an empty Chinese restaurant where I saw him sitting alone.

One half-eaten plate of spareribs beside an empty bottle of beer.

•

Often I find myself falling for men who cannot handle themselves. I watch them become their own shadows.

Out of sight, out of mind.

Some men climb out of my mind as if they were fleeing a flooded sewer. They twist open my ear, a wrought-iron gate, to scamper down my neck or up across my forehead.

The stink on them may last for years.

The stink on me?

Tiny indelible footprints heading off in every direction.

•

At a dinner party I am told I sound just like a famous comedienne. Around the table, my friends nod to note their agreement.

I have never found her funny, and I tell them this.

They say

See! You sound just like her—

•

In the state park just off Route 146, a man has been showing his penis to women.

I want to take a look!

On the way there I drive past The Rustic, the drive-through movie house where I saw my first porno with my third boyfriend, Steve, who got arrested later that same summer for stealing a human head from Kellett Cemetery.

He claimed he found it at the edge of the river and cleaned it with bleach and peroxide before deciding to use it as a bong.

I'm not kidding—

•

You know, I was surprised as the rest of you when she walked in carrying the baby.

Not just a baby, but a baby with two heads!

•

My sister called, checking to see if I was feeling normal. I read her a section from my essay "In Search of the Face." I said she could decide for herself.

Just then she was almost killed by a Detroit Transit bus coming down the wrong side of the road.

The bus driver was searching for seniors making out in the park after dark.

He wanted to make sure everyone got home safely.

He wanted to make sure everyone was using protection.

•

My first night alone in the house, I heard sobbing coming from the basement. When I got down there, I noticed the doorframe to the fruit cellar had been bricked shut.

I grabbed a sledgehammer from the wall of tools Mr. Melikian left when he sold me the place.

I struck at the wall until I made a hole big enough to hear a voice.

It was a face.

I took off my dress, handed it to him to wipe his tears, then brought him to my kitchen.

Asked if he wanted something to eat.

Two scrambled eggs.

•

A red balloon trapped in the branches of a tree outside my office window.

Two boys walking home without coats.

Pointing up to the balloon being tossed by March wind, one boy says to the other,

That's my tongue.

•

You can sing along—

•

Thursday night, driving to pick up dinner: one Chinese vegetable soup, one shrimp egg roll, please—

A boy standing in the middle of the road gives the finger

to his friend who shouts from the top balcony of a rob-in's-egg-blue triple-decker house.

I slow down, let the boy hurry to the sidewalk. As I pass him, he makes a motion with his hips to suggest having sex with my car.

His gesture, a poor articulation of seduction, makes me lonely, so I park at the corner, get out, beckon him to come over.

Facing the passenger-side rearview. I move my pelvis as if scooping ice cream.

I tell him

This is how you wear it down—

and really put my ass into it.

•

Something obvious is loneliness, how it always talks about itself in the third person. It says:

Oh never mind, you know what it says—

•

In my hometown a man offered an undercover police officer T-bone steaks in exchange for sex.

Because he didn't have any on him, he promised to pay the next day—

By the way, *solicitation* also means *to seek to obtain by persuasion.*

And the allure of humility plus gusto is often underestimated.

By the way, his mugshot made the 11 p.m. local news.

As if to say, when you are bartering sex for meat, there's no messing around.

You have got to pay up front.

•

Turns out my friend found her baby on the steps of the Laundromat she works at in Brooklyn.

I couldn't help myself and had to ask

How do you know whom to love?

I said (not leaving well-enough alone)

If two heads, then which face?

•

Follow the bouncing ball.

•

My neighbors made a list of improvements they thought I should make to my home and also let me know that my hair was in need of some work.

To excuse their cruel scrutiny, they brought steaks to sear on my mini-grill.

So we were all sitting around in the backyard chewing the fat when they started to take notes on what's wrong with my face.

•

Stand-up is harder than you think.

My first joke had a long lead-in about a businessman on

a trip to some foreign port of call with a few changes I made due to the fact that the joke is offensive to anyone named Wendy and has a usual overemphasis on the penis.

It went like this

A man, far away from home, discovered his worst fear to be true—that compared to most men in the world he was, in fact, very small.

Nobody laughed. So I told it again.

•

Something obvious is also regret, how it suggests there might have been any other way to go than this.

•

Grand Central Station, under the clock at the information booth, my friend waited to introduce her new baby to her mother.

While watching the broken clock, my friend held her daughter close—I am sure of that—

but she did not notice when one of her baby's heads rolled off.

•

Imagine you loved anyone. In the morning, you might wake up, think of all the dances you learned last night, but not a step comes back to you. Even your walk seems massive and zero. This is when you realize your body is still tucked safely inside someone else's, as it has always been.

Still, you do move.

•

While I was waiting out the dryer cycle in the Laundromat with Call-Me-Mary from Dublin (no joke), who didn't like to wash her elderly neighbor's intimate apparel in her own machine, my friend came in with her baby.

I said

Aren't you missing someone?

Call-Me-Mary said

What happened to the other head?

My friend said we were mistaken, her daughter had always been an average baby. Just one face.

•

I am waiting outside the train station for a friend to arrive from Chicago. A taxi driver throws old bread to pigeons that gather outside the vestibule.

From his car he watches passengers hurry in, hurry out. No one smiles.

A girl of maybe five or six years, who looks too small to be alone, carries a bright red backpack and looks as if she is about to tell him something—

He thinks he recognizes her but from where?

As so often is the case between strangers who might love each other, nothing happens between them.

The girl enters the train station and finds her way down to the tracks. She boards a train. She knows where she is going.

The taxi driver puts an older man's suitcase in the trunk of his cab.

The older man is embarrassed to have needed help, the driver pretends not to have noticed.

•

I am cleaning my glasses when a man I've never met rings my doorbell. I open it, and he says

You know me?

I think I recognize the face, so I say

Come on in. Can I get you a drink?

He confesses how many times he meant to pick up the phone and call, but hopes I've been getting news he was alright, not just alright but doing fantastically well—

He asks if I've seen his picture on the cover of any magazines at the grocery store, and I do think he smells a bit like the grocery store.

He asks if I still miss him, and I say

Out of sight, out of mind.

And so he goes on and on about how hard it has been to be far from home, on and on about how hard it is to remember the dances he learned last night—

He tells me

I thought you were someone else.

He tells me he's been looking for me for years, but now that he's here he can't recall why.

That's when I push him toward the door as if to say

Hey man, I've got no time to chat about how you got lost. I've got my own regrets, my own suckers to blame.

•

Back when I was a little whore, I left my tongue in some teen-aged boy's trousers or drawers.

A soft bulge near the crotch.

In order to say "trousers" or "drawers" I had to go back and get it.

•

My sister calls from the shopping mall. She is audition-
ing talent for her television show, *Super Singers*.

She says there's a teenaged girl with the best voice she's
ever heard who looks a lot like me. She could even be
my daughter, and she's singing this song I love.

If the girl makes the cut, she could compete on a live
local broadcast once a week. Win ten thousand dollars
or a red convertible.

The girl looks at the prompt on the monitor, tries to
recall how the words should fit together, but they fall
hard in all the wrong places like a fistful of rice or pen-
nies thrown at a window.

•

My friend, who works at the Laundromat, who *always*
buttons cuffs, spots stains and double-checks for loose
change, was shaking out wrinkles before the dryer
cycle.

One pair of khaki shorts, a soft bulge near the crotch.

Shit—

she said, reaching into the pocket.

Another handful of tiny, drowned men

•

By the way, *to find* means *to recover something lost* and *to come upon by accident.*

As if to say wherever you've left your head, it might still be thinking of you.

Multiply/Divide

1

I had been told it was my duty to multiply, but I had no plan to reveal this once I set out on the long, solitary drive to the sea. Though illegal to travel in my condition, I felt in control of my emotions. That is to say, I felt the aspiration to take up space. You might have been able to tell this from the message sent before I left. You were right in suspecting this trip was personal. An attempt to cast grudges aside.

2

You had judged me for being unable to see my solitary condition as temporary, but you had also made me breakfast one thousand times. Your affection had been platonic and constant as doubt. You had interpreted my problems as feminine, a quandary of proportions. You said to claim status as victim meant to separate myself from power. I got confused while thinking through types of degradation. In anger, I burst into four more of myself.

3

I did not see as the others with me saw. Not long on the road before I realized. Those with me vied for my attention, shared feelings inspired by exaggerations of their potency. Our repetition failed to impress us, too. Because we had not yet learned to reveal what we wanted from each other, we grew practiced in distraction.

4

Did we see ourselves advancing toward memories? We didn't want to admit we needed ourselves. We didn't want to confess we planned to distract ourselves from the aggression we felt toward strangers. Who looked at us as if we demanded to be hurt. Although at times trusting and faithful.

5

By nature our nervous system errs, is subject to defect. We are born in discomfort then want what we cannot do for ourselves. Not even for each other.

6

Games we played while driving: We imitated each other's feelings to try to understand us. We kept silent as a sign of approval or rejection. We invented our origins and practiced withholding affection. Every body reminded us of our distrust of the others.

7

Some of us wanted to ask us how we were doing but hesitated for lack of confidence. After four more hours of travel, resentment grew between us. We believed the offending party was that one or the other one. Our silences felt colder than the few words we managed to share, as every time we turned to forgive us, we were confronted by our face.

8

We heard ourselves kissing and moaning in the backseat and realized our injury was acting up. Maybe triggered by the weather. At an urgent care center we were advised to suspend our trip or risk permanent disability. The doctor gave us an armful of bandages, urging us to put them wherever we thought they would do the most good. At the very least, she cautioned, stop moving for a week. Out of respect for our ambition, we tore up the map before getting back on the road.

9

We did not arrive at the sea. You greeted our return with a lecture about how we would all have to share the space. As if we were too many. Of course, we hit back. The first blow landed on your jaw as if we had meant to disarm you. Believe me, we were shocked at how fast our fists got away from us. You had accused us of indulging in introspection, of oozing too much sentiment. We could have claimed violence was entirely our fault, but you would have seen through that.

10

You said you were always on the verge of discovering better women. Though we had become very desirable on the road due to being in constant company of each other. Not to aggrandize. All kinds of people had wanted us. Some had wanted to be us.

11

The more days we spent together, the more we disagreed about who was to blame for our misdirection. We still wanted to travel, so we rubbed at our injury all afternoon. An attempt to reclaim astonishment. We tried not to think of a single one of us as unfinished. We studied other fictions to understand what had made us so angry. We looked through books for evidence of our arrival. All the stories about when we fell in love or died. So many endings.

The Personal

I FIND OTHER PEOPLE to be more interesting than me, and in their company I can lose the loneliness that interferes with my expectations of adventure and opportunity. I am drawn to intimate stories, especially accounts of suffering or disadvantage, because they help me to understand the risks in being a person. To hear an account of the personal is a curious phenomenon, because for me, the tale must reflect on my own experience to feel relevant. The story must engage my empathy by creating a space for me to witness and recognize. An account of the personal illustrates an evolving consciousness, one that might be instructive even though it is neither fixed nor certain. The personal must be true, though that does not mean historically accurate.

To write the personal uncomplicates history, gives it a theme and direction. The speaker's demeanor during the telling alters the past. To share the personal is to pay homage to optimism, to the idea that one has the same opportunity to rewrite the past as one does to be bound by it. The effect is spectacle or theatre, both essential means for filling empty space.

Beginners to the stage, please.

One night when coming home late from a bookstore I worked at in Washington, DC, I parked my car a block from my apartment. A man approached. He gestured that I should roll my window down, and when I refused, he grabbed at my door, which fortunately was still locked. I managed to maneuver the car out of the parking space, and he jumped in his car to follow me as I sped down the street. I turned the corner and found another spot three blocks from my apartment, then ran though two alleys to get to my front door.

Even when I could not escape, I have been lucky. I avoided the groping aggressions of a high-school football player by sputtering out a warning that my parents, who were sleeping upstairs, would surely wake if I screamed. He left, seeming somewhat embarrassed for having tried anything at all.

When I lived in Los Angeles, I used to run before work. One morning, I was assaulted by a man dressed as a house painter. He came up behind me on a bicycle just as I was cresting the steep hill up North Western Avenue at Los Feliz Boulevard. He pushed me against a wrought-iron fence, rubbed his hands all over my buttocks, and tried to drag me into the bushes. I screamed and managed to push him off. I was surprised when he jumped on his bike to speed away. Rage or adrenaline made me chase him. I shouted to other joggers on the path to stop him, but they looked at me with disdain and suspicion. At that point, I still had about two and a half miles to go, so I picked up my run again, though I was crying and shaking. About a half mile down the road, I saw my assailant standing at the edge of a driveway facing the traffic on the busy street, pants down to his ankles, masturbating. He looked at me but did not stop pleasuring himself. I sprinted the rest of the way home.

•

My father's father was from Belize, and I suspected he was part Mayan, though my speculation would never be confirmed. The only evidence that supported my estimation was my birthmark, a blue nevus mole, rumored to be common amongst native people there. My mole, about the size of a dime, was on my back-side until a dermatologist removed it as a precaution during my last year of college. That same season, I ended up pregnant by a boyfriend I was fairly certain was not in love with me. I was not bothered by his intermittent affection as I had already experienced disappointment in love.

I'll admit I spent a lot of my twenties and thirties in intimate relationships with men who weren't in love with me yet didn't want me to date other people, either. I am not sure what to call that kind of condition, but it made me feel stupid. Later I learned to address my failure in sensibility by ending relationships in which a person wanted to share their feelings but not their body with me.

My pregnancy ended in an early miscarriage, but I was bereft for more than a year. Though I had begun graduate school, instead of talking about my feelings with potential new friends at a bar called The Chanticleer, I drank alone in my apartment to avoid confessing my sadness or sleeping with anyone who was gentle. I avoided people to my best ability until their burgeoning affection turned to indifference or hostility.

Graduate school was difficult for me because I was still depressed. Though I always completed the required reading, I often would fixate on the narrative contradictions I could not reconcile. During large discussions, questions would get stuck in my mouth. In that environment, a long pause sounded like hesitation or uncertainty, which seemed to convey I had no idea what I was talking about. I did not fare better with my written assignments. I liked to do fieldwork and interviews, but as I was studying literature I was advised to avoid primary source material because it could not be vetted. A few professors refused to work with me because they didn't believe I was capable of completing the degree.

One time I was asked to chauffeur a visiting literature professor from a southern university for the weekend. I drove him around campus and to and from his functions. Though he was more than thirty years my senior, we had similar critical concerns. Our exchange enlivened me. A few weeks after our first meeting, he mailed me an envelope of articles, which I found quite helpful. I called to thank him, and he asked me to meet him for a weekend affair at a hotel in New York City. When I refused, he cussed me out, told me my research was mediocre and that I would never succeed in academia.

In the personal, something about the word "I" intimates youth or, at the very least, youthful aspiration. Mishaps narrated in the first person tend to be more compelling for listeners, even though the "I" strives to keep the character distant and somewhat unknowable. Perhaps this is because the "I" always resides in the past, no matter how actively she speaks in present tense.

One looks back with a narrowed focus, a spotlight on the self imagining isolation in a crowd of potential companions.

•

I still wince when I remember ninth-grade girls calling me out for sitting at the lunch table with boys. The name "slut" stuck. In my sweater dresses and red high-heeled pumps with long, fake pearl necklaces or miniskirts and plunging V-neck sweaters with patterned turtlenecks, I was maturing conspicuously. Things didn't change once I switched to wearing men's flannel shirts and jeans. By then I was sexually active and quite proud of my developing skills in that area.

Would it be too personal for me to say that I grew less confident about sex as I got older, in part due to a number of disappointing relationships in which I was criticized for being too sexual or not sexual enough in the eyes of my romantic partner? There were many nights I behaved like I had no idea what I was doing— for instance, one evening in my difficult first marriage, I narrowly avoided bringing two English soccer coaches home with me, though I did buy them a last round of drinks before slipping out of the bar. By the time I reached my apartment, I was weeping myself back into another sinus infection.

After my marriage failed, I worried about my status as the lonely *divorcée,* a negative connotation reinforced by my father's habit of raising his eyebrows whenever he spoke the word. I tried to blend in by mowing my lawn and planting seasonal shrubs and flowers. I chatted with neighbors across the street who invited me over for tea or a glass of wine in the evening. They spoke of their courtship thirty years ago, how they struggled to have children and how driving a truck up and down I-95 as a couple strengthened their bond. Once they confessed their concern that a lot of black people were moving into the neighborhood, and I reminded them that I was black. To this they responded, *But you don't seem black.*

Sometimes I would get so lonely I would mastur-bate all day. The longest episode lasted for four days. I didn't answer the phone, go to the market, or visit friends. My pleasure dwindled with each orgasm until the whole exercise felt like planting seedlings into potting soil. When I told my therapist about it a week later, he asked—didn't I have a friend I could call when I was having those sort of feelings? A friend with whom to enjoy a brief affair? I told him I didn't, and that was the truth.

I got used to drinking at home because if I went out I might accidentally fuck a stranger and I had never successfully managed my one-night stands. Because I had evolved into a "good listener" some of these entanglements went on for years. By my mid-thirties, it became clear that these relationships were more about me wanting to be understood than sex though I can't think of one time in which I was successful in explaining this.

•

My behavior confused many others. Once I attended a party at the Argentinian Embassy in New York. Though I studied Spanish in college, I found it impossible to speak to people even as I was being introduced. Silence, without sound or air, prevented me from reaching the first syllable, in either language. After a few failed attempts at chitchat, I retreated to the coatroom. For the rest of the night my dear friend, who was not fazed by my awkwardness, brought me empanadas along with a stream of new people to meet. When we left the party I could not explain to him why I chose to sit amongst a pile of damp coats rather than talk with strangers.

The personal requires abjection so specific to the "I" that the only way to make it tangible is for the speaker to exaggerate her character. This can be accomplished by embellishing certain events in her life while leaving other details out. The audience anticipates its own likelihood to misperceive the personal due to a natural distance from the speaker and is forced to recognize how poorly the facts add up. While they wonder what these confessions are leading up to, the speaker lets slip some detail she will not be able to take back.

I did not make this choice consciously, but to hide my stutter, I got in the habit of starting sentences over again when I got stuck. I got in the habit of starting sentences over whenever I had to speak in new or unfamiliar situations or if I had to reveal something I had not before spoken of. I had a habit of remaining silent until I couldn't bear to not be a part of the discussion, and then when I did speak, I let loose all the words I could think to say. I would talk for too long, and others would lose interest. I would lose track of what I meant to say but worry about making sure I completed my speech so that I would not have to talk again for a very long time.

My family had become so accustomed to my strange and halting speech patterns that they could not hear my disfluency. But I did not have to speak long before a speech therapist acknowledged he could hear instances in which I could not get the words out.

One of the ways I learned to hide my stutter was to spout brief halting phrases as if I was trying to figure out what to say. This kind of control was not always within my reach, especially when I was nervous or speaking to someone for the first time. I would often choose to speak in a flat tone, suggesting my lack of interest or displeasure.

My manner fails to invite further exchange, though I do wish you would stay a little longer.

The lights in the house flicker. Time to decide: to stay or to go?

In the end any disclosure of the personal becomes ordinary. But isn't this always the way with accounts of a life? Ultimately what matters is the sound of the speaker's voice drawing attention to the light behind the curtain as it goes up. The audience sees what signs might be revealed. How odd it feels to share space with strangers, each of us sitting shoulder to shoulder, facing the same direction. Everyone here and somewhere else at the same time.

Post-Logical Notes on Self-Election

The morning after Barack Obama was elected president of the United States, I stopped to chat with the security guard at the entrance to my school. He is from Côte d'Ivoire and said someday, maybe forty years from now, he will return home.[1] He imagines his grandchildren will ask him about that day, and he will say, *I was there. I saw it with my own eyes.* When we shook hands to signal my leaving, we held on to each other as if passing a message of gratitude between us.[2]

He whispered, *He is strong. Everywhere in the world the black man is not welcome. Everywhere he is feared, despised. He has had to be on his own. Who better to lead than him?*

According to a survey conducted by the social networking site OkCupid.com in 2009, black women received the fewest responses to online dating invitations even though they were most likely to respond to messages sent to them by a person of any race.[3] Curiosity about dwindling opportunities for black marriage inspired numerous commentaries in major newspapers. Discussions reflected certain regional anxieties. In the Northeast, the problem was deemed the failure of black women to emulate actresses or singers widely regarded as "hot."

Poor knowledge of geography is a clear mark of one's intention to stay put, especially in cities where the borders between eighborhoods are not visible to those who live elsewhere. Mapping is always an act of distortion, and the fact that some of us live on roads not yet written down means that we do not exist.[4] Alternatively, it means that we exist as placeholders for someone else.

By the time Obama hit the campaign trail in 2006, gentrification in Washington, DC, was already impacting its black community. A few poets attempted to write about the city's most important sites before they disappeared from memory, but so few people read poetry that those places vanished anyways.

An 1822 aerial drawing of the city made by H. C. Carey notes only the following locations: the Capitol, the Marine Hospital, the President's House, the Navy Yard, and Greenleaf Point. All spaces in between, where people would live, are marked by rows of little black rectangles, stacked atop each other.[5] The Potomac bends to accommodate the city's sharp edges.[6]

By the time Michael Jackson died in the summer of 2009, the word on the street was that times were getting tougher for everyone, especially for the black middle class.[7] The black middle class didn't have much to say in response since most were still focused on fleeing to the suburbs or anchoring the upper-class with realness. No longer is it shocking to report how many of us believed in the inevitability of a middle class, just as we believed in concepts of inequity like celebrity and minority, words used to confirm the diminishing value of our contributions.[8]

While advertisers and political pundits hurried to name upcoming trends in popular culture as "the new black," the old black continued its attempts to gain control over its image. This project was complicated by the sudden acceptance of the idea that "multi" constituted the fastest growing racial category to be listed on the census. Multi aroused suspicion in the orthodox, who refused to think in ways that distracted from their need to distance themselves from the rest of us.

Frantz Fanon wrote this about his 1952 transformation in consciousness as if he anticipated what many of us would be seeking in a multicultural society: "I came into this world imbued with the will to find a meaning in things, my spirit filled with the desire to attain to the source of the world, and then I found that I was an object in the midst of other objects. Sealed into that crushing objecthood, I turned beseechingly to others. Their attention was a liberation, running over my body suddenly abraded into nonbeing, endowing me once more with an agility that I had thought lost, and by taking me out of the world, restoring me to it."[9] [10] In other words, a kind of freedom existed in being out of place. In order to take up space one needed to keep moving.

Thank goodness the technological means by which we could justify and express our narcissism was available on hand-held devices by the time most people recognized that their needs outweighed everyone else's. Missives on social status and desire could be broadcast twenty-four hours a day with minimal censorship or editing. Through this process of inventing our public face, our name became our brand, and we showcased our belief system each time we broadcasted our taste.

These are the names of the men who signed the Constitution on September 17, 1787: George Washington, Benjamin Franklin, James Madison, Alexander Hamilton, Gouverneur Morris, Robert Morris, James Wilson, Charles Pinckney, Charles Cotesworth Pinckney, John Rutledge, Pierce Butler, Roger Sherman, William Samuel Johnson, James McHenry, George Read, Richard Bassett, Richard Dobbs Spaight, William Blount, Hugh Williamson, Daniel of St. Thomas Jenifer, Rufus King, Nathaniel Gorham, Jonathan Dayton, Daniel Carroll, William Few, Abraham Baldwin, John Langdon,

Nicholas Gilman, William Livingston, William Paterson, Thomas Mifflin, George Clymer, Thomas FitzSimons, Jared Ingersoll, Gunning Bedford Jr., David Brearley, John Dickinson, John Blair, Jacob Broom, William Jackson.[11]

According to federal data, 539 white and 851 black juveniles committed murder in 2000. By 2007, the number of whites changed only slightly while for blacks the number increased to 1,142. Though murder rates in general had been much lower than in recent years, the number of younger blacks who became victims of murder also went up.[12] [13]

During the weekend of April 18–20, 2008, at least twenty-nine shootings took place within the city of Chicago.[14] Five people died. A majority of those targeted were young African American and Latino males. So much violence in the land of Lincoln meant we were not done hashing out who still owed whom for work undervalued, especially in economies where wealth was earned by showing no fear of death. In the months that followed, one Chicago paper began printing maps indicating where murders occurred each week.[15]

In the impoverished community of Central Falls, RI, police officers arrested nondocumented workers from local businesses to fill jail cells.[16] The more prisoners, the more subsidies the city received from the federal government. To sort out the criminals from the victims in this equation requires narrowing one's perspective to the vanishing point, the place where two paths converge.

Cartographers would often climb to great heights surrounding the city they were depicting in order to put the landscape in perspective. They also knew maps would sell better when cities appeared to be endlessly busy. Everyone hustled across a landscape of endless productivity. Thus a feature of the bird's-eye map was misrepresentation of scale.

Most maps don't make clear why the colors picked to represent the individual states, municipalities, and communities fail to bleed into each other.[17]

In California, Proposition 8, said to "protect marriage," was voted in favor of by a majority of citizens.[18] Early reports attributed the success of this measure to homophobia in the African American community, inspired by religion and parochialism. This analysis was another way, albeit subtle, that black people were characterized as a subset of humanity, content with negating the vastness of our own lived experience.

Some of the first states to legalize gay marriage included Vermont, New Jersey, Connecticut, New Hampshire, Massachusetts, Iowa, and Maine, despite the once-popular Defense of Marriage Act passed in September of 1996. It attempted to prevent individual states from defining marriage as anything other than a "legal union between one man and one woman." Those of us who had been through a marriage asked why so much time was spent defining what marriage *wasn't*—when no one could say for certain what it *was*.

From the first moments she came to the attention of the public, Michelle Obama appeared in several places she was not expected to be seen: in the fashion house, in the garden, at the VA hospital, and in the poetry section of the bookstore. For many Americans who still did not comprehend how many innovations they had already failed to take note of, her presence disrupted the tradition of ignoring black women. Up until this point the black woman had functioned, whether as cartoon, caretaker, chimera, or Oprah, as the empathetic presence in fictions of racial harmony and desire, capable of the kind of understanding and forgiveness too sentimental to be heroic.[19] For generations she played fulcrum in the evolution of whites with privilege to a liberal consciousness. After Michelle she had become oddly untenable, multiple, and divergent.

At the time when so many changes began to unravel the way we thought about America, these were some of the poorest cities: Gary, IN; Hartford, CT; Camden, NJ; St. Louis, MO; Edinburg, TX; Flint, MI; Cleveland, OH; Buffalo, NY; Milwaukee, WI; New Orleans, LA; El Paso, TX; Baltimore, MD; Toledo, OH; Stockton, CA; Lowell, MA; Tulsa, OK; Detroit, MI; Memphis, TN; Newark, NJ; Barstow, CA; Youngstown, OH; and Brownsville, TX.

For about two months, a lot of people were on the verge of saying racism was over. Then Oscar Grant got shot in the back in a BART station in Oakland, CA, during the early morning hours of January 1, 2009.[20] It would be easier to deal with conflict if everyone thought about the same things, but the injuries we suffered from most were felt personally not philosophically.[21]

While considering hard facts about the life of Richard Wright, James Baldwin wrote this about racism: "One is always in the position of having to decide between amputation and gangrene."[22] [23] A kind of death is implied, localized at first—how the body learns to absorb the fear of others.

In 1845, Frederick Douglass wrote about the pursuit of freedom, "In coming to a fixed determination to run away, we did more than Patrick Henry, when he resolved upon liberty or death.[24] With us it was a doubtful liberty at most, and almost certain death if we failed."[25] When it was our moment to act, many of us still wanted to run, but to where we did not know.

One morning two musicians on the subway complained about how no one looks a stranger in the eye anymore. They claimed everyone was afraid of each other. I wanted to shout, *People aren't interested in anyone other than themselves*, but didn't think anyone cared enough to listen.

Amongst the Civil Rights generation, the name of the virus was still being whispered in the same way our parents muttered "cancer" before each of them was diagnosed with it. By the time African Americans comprised 49% of those newly infected with HIV, the CDC recommended that testing be mandatory for all African Americans living in certain cities. This approach revealed the mistaken impression that high rates of transmission in black communities were the result of bad desire rather than evidence of a lack of economic opportunity, access to health care, and emotional support for those suffering from lower self-esteem.[26]

One of the biggest challenges in mapmaking has to be accurately representing those places with the least growth. The mapmaker faces the problem of determining what to show. Potential use or lack thereof? What good is a road no one travels on? Is a neighborhood no one lives in still a community?

These were some of the blackest cities in the US: Washington, DC; East St. Louis, IL; Detroit, MI; Baltimore, MD; Jackson, MS; Birmingham, AL; Richmond, VA; Memphis, TN; Gary, IN; Atlanta, GA; Oakland, CA; Louisville, KY; Baton Rouge, LA; Jersey City, NJ; Mobile, AL; Chicago, IL; Norfolk, VA; Philadelphia, PA; Cincinnati, OH; Charlotte, NC; and Rochester, NY.[27]

The value of the echo is that it teaches listening, though we all know that, at times, throwing your voice out there is the only way to deal with obstructing surfaces. One clear echo was the blackest and the poorest at the same time.

It didn't matter that critics still debated the relevance of hip-hop in the broader culture; clearly it had already transformed the way people mix it up around the world. But if anybody could be president, this was the beginning of the end of the culture of distraction or what we used to call "celebrity."[28] [29]

The weekend of President Obama's inauguration, we rode down to DC on the train. People waved welcome signs along the tracks in South Philadelphia, PA. Days earlier in New York, NY, a plane had crash-landed in the Hudson River. No one knows why everyone survived other than the fact that some luck is unfathomable.[30]

A young boy sitting with his white mother on the train considered the map in his hands easy reading. Most people didn't stare at him, except the few who wondered how he came to be so good with directions. The boy, too confident to notice their attention, pointed out the attractions in each city along the route. Through his comprehension of geography, the boy told all studying him, *You have no idea who I am.*

In his inaugural address, President Obama referenced George Washington and Thomas Paine with respect to one of the most difficult times in the American Revolution: "Let it be told to the future world that in the depth of winter, when nothing but hope and virtue could survive, that the city and the country, alarmed at one common danger, came forth to meet it."[31] We came forth as well, everyone out in the cold, awaiting direction on our next move.

One of the hardest concepts about America to reckon with had been that it would always be a land of fractured allegiances.[32] Demands for equality and justice were unending, and the means by which we sought them defined how close we were to winning or losing our ideals. It seemed there would always be a struggle for America to become itself. No doubt that there were times when we all got tired of talking about it.

Those who marched from Selma to Montgomery, AL, in 1965 caught rancor from the weapons, hoses, and dogs turned on them.[33] For years after that, there were those who might have died from disappointment but chose to spread their anger around like a virus.[34]

And there were those who let go of their anger because they wanted to live, but every step they took after that was just an inch or two below ground level.

Even though a tension between the city and country in the US had always played out in political debate, we were thankful that our dream for America still included both a community one could feel and a community one could see.[35] Making a justification for the further development of suburbs after the influence of a black middle class had been grossly over-stated, however, was much more difficult.

The men who signed the Declaration of Independence wrote this about the new democracy: "We mutually pledge to each other our Lives, our Fortunes and our sacred Honor," before there was any evidence that they would survive the act of treason. And while some of us knew that a willingness to commit treason is sometimes the truest test of a patriot, the faith it took to believe in America this time around required no less of a conviction. This was when we started to show up in person, all of us coming out in the cold looking for one face to remind us of where we could have been going, in what direction.

Notes

1. At the time of our conversation, approximately 25% of the residents of Côte d'Ivoire lived below the international poverty line. In Detroit, MI, unemployment rates were rising and would reach nearly 16.1% within six months. http://www.bls.gov/news.release/metro.nr0.htm

2. Occasional touching of coworkers was considered to be awkward except when the intimacy of the conversation already extended beyond what might be considered casual.

3. For additional insight, see http://blog.okcupid.com/index.php/your-race-affects-whether-people-write-you-back/

4. "Road" also implies a cut path, a lack of originality, a charted destiny, and the attempt to follow.

5. H. C. Carey, noted mapmaker, was the author of *Carey's School Atlas,* published in 1825, priced at one dollar plain and one twenty-five colored. Maps of the world—England, Scotland, Ireland, France, Spain, Italy, Germany, Asia, North America, United States, and South America—were contained therein.

6. http://www.davidrumsey.com/luna/servlet/detailRUMSEY~8~1~742~70016:Geographical,-Historical,-And-Stati

7. Michael Jackson (1958–2009) was an American enter-

tainer who was, at one time, the best-selling singer and composer of popular music worldwide. At the time he died, many claimed he had been the most popular celebrity of all time.

8. The "middle class" was said to be the social class between the lower and upper classes, though its precise boundaries were always difficult to define, especially in times of economic tumult. Eventually it became known as a temporary state through which one passed en route to the upper or lower classes rather than a position in which to maintain a lifestyle. The "black middle class" was a post-WWII invention created to relieve concern about the long-term effectiveness of coercive segregation.

9. Frantz Fanon (1925–1961) was a psychiatrist, philosopher, revolutionary, and author from Martinique, who was considered an expert on the psychological effects of racism and colonialism.

10. Fanon, *The Wretched of the Earth,* 109.

11. How many times is it possible to form the word "no" from these names as they are listed in order?

12. http://www.nytimes.com/2008/12/29/us/29homicide.html?_r=1

13. *Victims . . . of murder . . . went up . . .* this route to ascension seemed unnecessarily steep.

14. "At least six people have been shot to death and more than two dozen others wounded in shootings since Friday afternoon in Chicago. At one point 18 shootings had occurred in 17 hours." http://abclocal.go.com/wls/story?section=news/local&id=6091348

15. In 2009 *RedEye* tracked all murders that occurred in Chicago. "In every Thursday paper, *RedEye* will publish a map of the homicides from the previous week. This interactive map also will be updated weekly." "Tracking Homicides in Chicago: Homicide Map." *RED EYE.* http://homicides.red eyechicago.com/date/.

16. Bernstein, Nina. "City of Immigrants Fills Jail Cells with Its Own" *NY Times,* 26 December 2008. http://www.nytimes.com/2008/12/27/us/27detain.html?_r=1&scp=1&sq=rhode%20island%20central%20falls&st=cse

17. "To bleed" could imply falling in love, which might or might not play out as tragedy.

18. Proposition 8 was a ballot proposition against gay marriage that passed in the November 4, 2008, general election and went into effect the next day.

19. Oprah Winfrey (b. 1954) was a popular American media personality and entrepreneur whose brand included a television talk show, a production company, several magazines, a cable network, and many other successful projects. While her initial target audience was women in the US, her advice on personal challenges and ability to make anyone who appeared on her show famous appealed to almost everyone.

20. Oscar Grant, a twenty-two-year-old unarmed man, was shot by a BART officer in the Fruitvale BART station in Oakland, CA. When killed, he was in a submissive position. http://www.indybay.org/newsitems/2009/01/03/18558098.php

21. You know what we mean.

22. Richard Wright (1908–1960) was a writer born into a Mississippi family of sharecroppers. In 1927 he moved to Chicago, a city that would inform his most famous and controversial book, *Native Son.* James Baldwin (1924–1987) was a writer born in Harlem, whose work in essays, plays, and fiction documented the complexity of changes that came as a result of the Civil Rights Movement. His work also explored the complications of expressing sexuality within an African American community struggling for acknowledgment and validation in the larger society.

23. This metaphor is excerpted from "Notes of a Native

Son." Baldwin, James. "Notes of a Native Son" in Lopate, Phillip. *The Art of the Personal Essay: An Anthology from the Classical Era to the Present*. New York: Anchor, 1997, p. 603.

24. Patrick Henry (1736–1799) was a prominent, radical figure of the American Revolutionary War. In a speech given about patriotism in 1775, he shouted the phrase, "give me liberty, or give me death," which became a battle-cry for like minded individuals seeking to end British influence over the American colonies. The ratification of the Constitution, Henry served as the governor of the Commonwealth of Virginia for several terms.

25. Douglass, Frederick. *Narrative of the Life of Frederick Douglass*. New York: Signet, 1968. p. 57.

26. From the Centers for Disease Control website, "According to the 2000 census, blacks make up approximately 13% of the US population. However, in 2005, blacks accounted for 18,121 (49%) of the estimated 37,331 new HIV/AIDS diagnoses in the United States in the 33 states with long-term, confidential name-based HIV reporting." http://www.cdc.gov/omhd/highlights/2008/hfeb08.htm

27. Location, location, location!

28. Celebrity was a global cultural phenomenon that reached its peak during the first decade of the 21st century. Film and musical performers, along with hired agents and publicists, worked to hold a position in the center of the public eye. The attention they received, often inversely proportional to their talent (with a few notable exceptions), served as a distraction from the global consolidation of capital systems amongst a few key corporations whose influence, though not recognizably coercive, was similar or broader in scope than those ideological, transnational armies professing a desire to destroy or create influential nations.

29. Celebrities who attended the inaugural balls went with the expectation that they would be recognized for bringing

something distinctive to the party. But now that it appeared that anyone could be president, it mattered less that some of us could be pop icons.

30. This notable landing, called the "Miracle on the Hudson," was executed by a seasoned pilot, Captain Chesley "Sully" Sullenberger. After the crash, Sullyenberger testified before the National Transportation Safety Bureau about the danger of having so many inexperienced pilots in the air. http://www.usatoday.com/news/nation/2009-06-08-hudson_N.htm

Since the terrorist attacks of September 11, 2001, airlines had been faced with drastic cost-cutting measures in order to stay in business and as a result employed more overworked, underpaid, and novice pilots than ever before. http://abc news.go.com/GMA/BusinessTravelstory?id=4232878

31. http://www.nytimes.com/2009/01/20/us/politics/20text-obama.html

32. Because even before the statue arrived, we had called for the tired, poor, huddled masses yearning to breathe free, the wretched refuse of distant teeming shores, the homeless and tempest-tossed to come home to our lamp-lit golden door.

33. "On 'Bloody Sunday,' March 7, 1965, some 600 Civil Rights marchers headed east out of Selma on US Route 80. They got only as far as the Edmund Pettus Bridge six blocks away, where state and local lawmen attacked them with billy clubs and tear gas and drove them back into Selma. Two days later on March 9, Martin Luther King, Jr., led a 'symbolic' march to the bridge. Then Civil Rights leaders sought court protection for a third, full-scale march from Selma to the state capitol in Montgomery." http://www.nps.gov/his tory/nr/travel/civilrights/al4.htm

34. Cancer is not a virus and cannot be spread from person to person. Still, no one in the scientific or academic com-

munities could account for the frequency and virulence of it amongst the Civil Rights generation without speculating that at its root was either a long period of dormancy or transmission through political participation.

35. Many assumed "home" was where these imagined spaces converged.

Cowboy Horizon

THE WESTERN APPEARED as jagged mountain peaks, lush grasslands, smooth deserts, and astronomical canyons unspoiled by our good deeds, but it could not be found on any map. More important than its looks was how it made us feel. Who could blame anyone for wanting to see pictures of that landscape one thousand times?

In time we would make The Western a vacationland, but not before we learned to excel in violence. Following the shocks and twitches of our guns, we killed everyone we met, then we moved by wagon and horse onto plains to become a better version of ourselves. We sought a frontier at once easy to access and too remote, perilous and safe, wild and wholly predictable, with terrain that could be mastered by any committed novice. We set off in the direction of the little town that did not know our virtues were criminal.

We needed stories to keep us hopeful as we sought liberation from the cities, freedom from the throng of convoluted masses who crossed the Atlantic after us, those who spoke languages that could never blend with ours. We regaled each other with tales of killing on behalf of women, for the virtue of women, and for our right to win women. If women interrupted our expansion of ego, then we killed them, too. We had so much distance to cross back when we all were Men.

Because we could not reach the horizon without violence, we came to be intimate with anyone who interfered with our desire to be lonesome, to play out adolescent emotions through masculine adventures. To the south there was No Mexico, nothing but grasslands and desserts since 1524, not the plain on which the gods live, not the lake at the center of the moon.

It was our destiny to charge into Texas, to lob the first stones at Santa Anna. What better than a war to demonstrate our habit of "thinking big"? Our will manifested the states of Colorado, Wyoming, Nevada, Utah, Oklahoma, Texas, Arizona, New Mexico, and California.

•

To demonstrate peace, we buried shell casings amongst the mallow, clover, buckwheat, cactus, peppergrass, milkweed, and primrose that rose up to meet the sky at dusk, colors like brushfire yielding to a riverbank. We admired the patience of farmers, who grew crops subject to seasons and weather, and the ambitions of ranchers, who put as many or as few cattle as they liked on the prairie without care to what it did to the grasslands and swales.

Mountains and plains set the cameras rolling to better capture the distant terrain where we could be more removed from each other. From one town to the next, we searched for home through dust clouds and sagebrush. We willed ourselves to keep riding until we recognized it.

Our pistols answered the doubt of those who disagreed with us. Our confidence stretched on for years.

•

The frontier kept moving, so we rode on, aiming for the horizon. Because the land we trod on leaked oil, banks sent Professional Men to claim the territory for people who never worked it a single day in their lives. In time they cleared the farmers and ranchers from their settlements because neither made enough money to please the banks. They left us, the hired hands, to kick up dust.

Without the religion of work to shape us, we turned into Misfits. We spoke against the law, stormed the banks, and galloped alongside railcars with guns in hand. We drew fire from Professional Men who believed the pursuit of profit to be the only virtue, men who could not remember a time when money did not make the difference between the law and what was right.

As Misfits we had a code to help us maintain our honor, one we followed even when in peril:

A man must not smile and shoot.

A man must not make war when seated at the table with his enemy.

A man must not shoot an unarmed rival (unless the rival will never become White).

A man must not ambush the enemy.

A man must not fight on what is known to be neutral ground.

A man must crave isolation because at the end of the film, we leave love and our kin in spirit behind to ride alone through the glitter.

A man may null and void these points at any time.

•

Fog tumbled toward us after we crossed the Rockies into California, and we could not deny our relief from the drop in temperature. We wanted to see the water, and once we got close enough to hear it, we thought the sea offered infinite vistas, waves colliding in all directions. Some of us cursed at the water for so quickly changing our ambitions from dust to mist. Some of us said we should have rested at its edge and made the most out of being in that light. Some of us knew we should have headed back the way we came to take our punishment—which was to live amongst the others in cooperation.

We tried to forget our solitary stance, the need to wander from the crowds, the sound of the wind picking up gravel, the snakes stirring at the approach of horses. We tried to forget the canyons into which we shouted our names into nothingness, but we had no desire to cure our nostalgia.

Because we felt so lonesome, we believed every word we read. We did not know the Journalists had predicted war in order to sell more daily editions. Pictures in the newspapers of Cuba, Guam, Puerto Rico, and the Philippines sold us on a paradise still green for the taking.

•

Though we believed ourselves to be brave, the ocean was more celestial than we expected. We had no idea how to put ourselves at the center of it. Blame it on the current or wind, but when our ship pitched we nearly lost our guns to the water. Without a horse beneath us, our sense of balance was poor. Some nights we could not tell the difference between the earth and sky.

We were looking for war, in Pacific Nation after Pacific Nation. Because we never studied stories of shipwreck and ruin by ambition, we believed we were still novices in the ritual of battle. Once we landed ashore, we killed people to mark territories we would keep for ourselves—from the war to create the Insular Government in the Philippines, to the war to push North Korea back past the 38th Parallel. When we got confused about why we fought, we killed more people.

Our guns pointed to more picturesque landscapes we knew should be ours. Rough waves in the Luzon Strait sent us adrift toward the South China Sea and other points rising.

•

Our next landing took us to Vietnam. Twilight at the horizon cast a heroic glow over our story, so the Journalists couldn't help but follow us in. We let them walk with us around the green mountains buffered by clouds, over the loam-rich fields of humble bounty, past the moss-covered temples that closed the gap between heaven and exile. Palm trees rose infinitely.

In the war we wrangled these people into hamlets and hillocks we invented, though they told us their connection to the ground went generations deep. When they would not stay put, we killed them a million more times. They said their graves must be tended to in order to keep them from becoming wilderness. Talk of wilderness made us homesick for The Western so we called home to say, *Bring us back,* that we were done with fighting.

•

Maybe we had been dead for too long, but in the photographs the Journalists took of us we looked angry, as if we had just come to realize our valor had been squandered on war. Displeased with their reading of us, we picked up our pace. No one had answered our request to bring us home, so we sped up the killing, too, in the hope that we could finally get to the end of it. In time new planes approached the battlefields. We thought they had come for us, but they flew past where we stood with arms waving in the air, to bomb open the killing fields.

For years we watched planes fly west.

We were not privy to the talks between heads of state, but one day either a treaty was signed or truce was broken. In the fog, a pale light shone as a road unfurled toward us. Because it shimmered as if from heat, we did not realize it was made entirely of bones. When we set foot on it, we heard the sound of a million people crying out from pain and dislocation. We hesitated while standing in the shade of an enormous gnarled tree, on which a speaker played music loud enough to drown out their voices. Despite the din, we thought we heard them say every one of our names. But when we turned to each other for recognition, our faces filled with fear and confusion made it clear we had become ghosts for good.

Though they regarded us with tenderness and pity, not even the Journalists would have predicted that they would be the ones to write us home:

> Grunts slog through a swamp with confidence,
> as they have not yet been in battle. From his
> pocket, a young man pulls out a picture of a

woman turned away from the camera. She wears a white blouse and a short red skirt. Her beautiful legs appear to be set to start running. The grunt pushes the photograph of the woman back into his vest. Another soldier coughs deeply, the sound of infection. He struggles to keep up with the platoon. Each man has a quality about him that reveals youth: shoulders cut too narrowly, mottos inscribed on their uniform or helmet, a tendency to stare too long at anyone's face for recognition. Bullets whiz past. Some of the soldiers explode with wounds. One man succumbs as another dials for help. It seems like hours pass before the planes arrive to burn everything inside the perimeter. The soldier with the photograph has died, but his friend keeps the picture for himself. A soldier accepts the pilot's offer to ride back to base before realizing the chopper also carries casualties. They begin the work of closing eyes and bagging the dead. One day the soldier will write a book that explains how to survive as a man, which means how to forget all the places in which he claimed to become one.

Procedural

M. ALREADY KNOWS THAT, no matter how hard she does the job, there is something she wants that she will not get. She knows this is because one of the tasks at her job is to tell other people, *No matter how hard you do the job, there is something you want that you will not get.*

M. works hard at the call center all day and this is why she wants to come home to a house that feels like it has room enough for her tired body. All day she listens to clients complain about machines that broke. They ask her how is she going to fix it? But M. can't fix anything, she is not allowed to. So she promises to elevate the conversation to the manager and sends each voice away. At the end of the day, the sum of disappointments makes her knees and shoulders ache, but still she wants sex. Then she wants it wiped away. How much M. needs to rest depends on how accustomed she has come to feeling broken, but when she moves her body she remembers what doing the job has taken from her. She used to believe if she did the job hard enough, she would find satisfaction, that she could be more free from history than others, that she would come to be exempt from biology or poverty. When M. was younger, she used to throw darts at the sky without fear of gravity, but now she craves inertia, to be at rest.

M. picks up her dirty laundry, puts it into the machine, scrapes the food off the dishes, wipes down the bathroom sink and mirror because it is not enough to have a tidy house. She needs a clean house, too, so she can forget her own history. M. doesn't care if this means she must dissolve traces of herself, too, because she already suspects she does not have the right to exist anywhere. This insight came to her while doing the job every day. Why not turn on the television?

M. suffers through an episode:

VICTIM: I'm missing an ear.
DETECTIVE: Keep an eye out for the victim's ear.

VICTIM: If I hadn't been beautiful, the killer would never have noticed me.

DETECTIVE: Show us your body again. Piece by piece.

M. watches procedurals because she knows what to expect from them. A person is turned into a corpse. Detectives Woodward and Lafayette pursue the reasons. They help M. to understand the criminal's intentions. By the end of the show everyone can see that the dead are guilty for failing to predict what was coming to them.

In the courtroom scenes witnesses attempt to recall the moment of loss or disbelief. Stories flicker by, each one its own demonstration of tragedy:

Victim #2, a junior high school student, has been shot and abandoned by his mother in an emergency room.

Victim #3, who wears a trench coat and carries a briefcase, is discovered bleeding in the garage. She appears to have been stabbed, but no—a baby has been cut from her womb. Later on the infant's body is found in a nearby trash heap.

Victim #4, a small girl with curly brown hair and false teeth, is found inside a suitcase under the seat of a bus.

In her backyard, an elderly woman covers her negligee with a wool blanket as she talks on the phone to her philandering husband. Looking up at the night sky, she sees what she thinks is a dead animal in a tree. She shakes it, freeing Victim #5, a young woman in a maid's uniform whose face is gone.

•

Detective Woodward struggles to relate to other members of her squad, because, when we first meet her, she is not written well. In time she comes to have depression, too, perhaps after she kills a suspect for the first time. Eventually she will be assaulted, but no one knows when or how this will happen. She worries she has too much empathy for the victims, so she masks this with directness and a frequent look of incredulity, as if nothing she hears will be believed. Detective Lafayette used to be handsome, but ten years ago he betrayed his partner and sent him to jail. After that he gave in to a sadness so deep that his face will never recover. Detective Lafayette plays his despair comically to keep the story moving. He struggles to maintain boundaries between what he knows is right and the directives that come from the Chief and the Mayor. Secretly he wants to be Mayor because the Mayor is a liar and a thief, and rich.

•

After hours of watching detectives solve crimes, M. realizes she has more in common with the suspect than she thought. The suspect commits to doing the job every day, just like she does. The suspect was not looking to get in trouble, but trouble has been finding him all his life. The suspect suffered from a lack of understanding, though he tried to explain himself. The suspect pretended to be unaware that any crime has been committed, even the ones committed against him. It is in his inscrutable face that, at last, she recognized herself.

SUSPECT: I would never hurt that girl.
DETECTIVE: Help us help you.
SUSPECT: You've got this all wrong.
DETECTIVE: She had sex before she died.
SUSPECT: I don't even like guns!
DETECTIVE: The DNA confirms you were there.
SUSPECT: I thought she loved me.

•

When she opens the door to receive a delivery, Victim #117—a young woman who works obsessively on her computer—is grabbed and then thrown off the balcony of her apartment. The man killed her because he wanted her to stop sending messages to his best friend.

A movie star's wife, who suffers from low self-esteem, spends her day shopping at expensive boutiques where she treats the employees rudely. She is Victim #118, found poisoned in the shower. Her hairdresser, who often talked about her "secret boyfriend," killed her because she was in love with the victim's movie star husband.

Victim #119's body is found in the trunk of her car. Her husband, Victim #120, was hit in the head with a sculpture. Men from a child pornography ring killed them for discovering how a young girl disappeared.

•

Come on in, M. says—but she doesn't mean it. Most of the time, home is where she retreats to when she needs to protect herself from those who have not invited her in. Here is her nation of oneness. The door is a wall and so on.

So who comes knocking? A stranger, of course. One who should not enter the home unless she gives permission for him to do so. These are the conventions of mystery, what allows us to see danger coming before she does. Home stands in for the dweller's body. Or the house is clean, no body is here.

Come on in, she says—

•

The medical examiner's report notes great harm has been done to a body, trauma that left evidence of cruelty. No reason could justify the use of such force. The medical examiner declares the body a question, as the detectives speculate on the criminal's motivation. The medical examiner details the wounds without showing emotion, so everyone knows how much there is to see. They tell us not to stop and stare, urge us to keep going: *Move along, folks.*

The detectives broaden their search for suspects. Suddenly we are all implicated. How did we get so close to the crime scene? The body in our path, a stone. We step over it.

•

The cops look for a description of the suspect. Besides a general nervousness, an inability to contain emotion, the perpetrator, as yet, has no distinguishing marks or traits. Detective Woodward feels like she knows the kind of character who did it. She has seen this sort of thing go down before, back when she worked in Philadelphia or Baltimore or St. Louis. Detective Lafayette, still traumatized by the damage done to the body, keeps thinking of his wife who cheated on him with a lawyer or a judge. His wife took their son and moved in with her parents who live on the outskirts of Philadelphia or Baltimore or St. Louis.

The medical examiner reports a new finding. The killer left a kind of signature on the body, one hard to read until the toxicology reports came back. The killer's mark is kept secret from the press, to prevent disruptions in the investigation. The medical examiner feels particularly attractive after having uncovered such an important piece of evidence.

He spends all weekend in the morgue because warm weather inspires impatience, provokes violence. Bodies keep coming in, but this does not upset the medical examiner as his job is to tally up the flesh. He wants a number that makes it clear why he has worked his whole life. The medical examiner does the job because it makes him feel respected though burdened by knowledge of pain.

The medical examiner goes home after a long day and can't talk to anyone about what he has seen because everything he has seen is a secret. He goes for a walk and notices the trees will bloom any day. He thinks of their flowers but mostly the pollen that will fall everywhere. He rubs his eyes in anticipation of irritation.

MEDICAL EXAMINER: It's been a long winter.
DETECTIVE: This is the season of sure things.

MEDICAL EXAMINER:	That's what I used to think. Then I found this clump of clay on the heel of the boot.
DETECTIVE:	Origin?
MEDICAL EXAMINER:	Probably early America.
DETECTIVE:	Somebody lied to us.

•

A father comes home to find his son is missing and goes out looking for him. Three men bring him to his knees in front of an open grave. His son kneels beside him. Victims #233 and #234.

A man notices bandages and alcohol spilling out of a grocery bag another man is carrying. He follows the man to a small house, in which a young woman is bleeding from a gunshot wound. He touches her cheek and tells her to keep breathing. She is Victim #235.

A man decides to kill the detective who arrested his father. The assassin hides in the detective's apartment. When the detective comes home he notices the light he always leaves on in the kitchen has burned out. Wait, the bulb was unscrewed. Wait, there is someone in the apartment who shouldn't be there. Victims #236 and #237?

•

M. does the job hard all day and this is why she wants to come home to a house that feels big enough for her tired body to rest haphazardly. Sometimes M. forgets how much time she has lost, but at the end of the day a sense of resignation returns when she thinks of tomorrow and doing it all over again. The truth is there is no way to win the world if she plays by the rules. Even though being good at her work means she might be able to get away with more missteps, crossing those lines will never add up to a clean house.

•

Detective Woodward explains that the reason they have come to M.'s door is because they think she can help them understand what happened to the woman. Detective Lafayette tells her it would be great if she could just come down to the station with them. In the interrogation room, a detective she hasn't seen before gets her a cup of coffee and sits with her in silence. This detective is new to the department, but a seasoned interrogator. Let's call her Detective Bloomfield, and she appears to be staring down the wall. When Detective Woodward comes back into the room, pulls out the chair and sits down, Detective Bloomfield stands behind him against the door. M. has seen this conversation three hundred and thirteen times before. She wonders how they will get her to confess. How long can her will to hold out last? For a moment, she enjoys the rush of adrenaline, but she is also bored with the plot.

On the other side of the two-way mirror, Detective Lafayette watches the conversation between the suspect and Detective Woodward turn sour. Detective Bloomfield exits the interrogation room then returns with a stack of papers. Detective Woodward reads from the evidence. Detective Lafayette trusts his partner to keep her composure throughout the interrogation. He wants to enter the room, but he waits for his cue. At some point Detective Woodward indicates the suspect has run out of things to say. M. swears she knows nothing of the victim, of violence, but she can't prove it because the detectives keep finding her in their evidence. They show her pictures of bodies. How will she ever forget what she has seen?

M. and Detective Bloomfield go back and forth in the room, maybe for half the day. Soon it is time for the cleaner to tend to the interrogation rooms. Normally he begins his shift by wiping down the tables, then mopping the floors. He is not too careful about how he cleans these spaces because they soon will be dirty again. Still he feels a particular sense of obligation when it comes to the table and the chairs. These need to be done better than the rest. He believes a suspect sitting in a clean chair and at a clean table will feel more confident, say what is really on her mind even if it means there will be punishment.

M. admits she enjoyed watching the victim suffer. It felt good to transfer the discomfort of knowing she is unimportant to someone else. All the complaints she endured at the call center made it clear that other people wanted her to share their anger, too. Why blame her for trying to do this cruelty better?

M. tells the detective she couldn't help the violence, though she knows it is not true. She claims fate put the victim in the way of the changes she wanted to make: an obstacle. What else could she do? She writes this story on the lined yellow paper.

Eventually the detectives remove her from the interrogation room. Now it is time again for the cleaner. Once he does this job, he will head home to shower. He doesn't want to be reminded of feelings that come from all he has seen today. So he makes his home so clean he can forget himself. He suspects he does not have the right to exist anywhere. His insight comes from studying the boxes where they keep the people. Why not turn on the television?

Manhattanville, Part Two

EACH TIME MY SON and I walk to the Fairway grocery store on 12th Avenue and 132nd Street, we grab a copy of the weekly *Manhattanville in West Harlem Campus Plan,* the update on the university's expansion, from a plexiglass box on the plywood fence separating us from the new campus's construction site. Fairway sits on the west side of the Riverside Drive Viaduct, an ornamental steel roadbed erected in 1900, composed of a series of arches that cascade into the vanishing point. The viaduct was created to allow its travelers to bypass the grimy, noisy shops of Manhattanville and take in an elevated view of the Hudson River as they made their way north into the hillsides of upper Manhattan. *Viaduct* was one of my son's first words, and I suspect this was due to our weekly trips to the market, during which we often stopped at the new West Harlem Piers to admire the George Washington Bridge.

I have been collecting these weekly updates since my son was a baby because the heart of my neighborhood is changing from a gritty, industrial corridor to an illuminated city of glass. Buildings I have grown accustomed to seeing every day have been dismantled, and streets have disappeared into a long, flat hole out of which the new campus will rise while I, like many other residents of Manhattanville, will be left standing at the outskirts of possibility.

When I compare the "What Is Happening" sections in the update to the previous week's, I notice progress has been made on the largest building, including installation of the glass façade windows, partitions of the internal space, and masonry work on the lower levels. Though the flyers tell me what to expect each week at the site, endless pipe and drain work sounds like an ancient clash between maintenance and entropy.

Such conflicts are not new for the area. In September of 1776, a buckwheat field near the southern edge of what would become Manhattanville served as the stage for the Battle of Harlem Heights, a turning point in the Revolutionary War. Following a devastating loss at the Battle of Long Island in August, the Continental Army took shelter in Harlem at the northern end of Manhattan. Shortly after George Washington arrived, he sent Thomas Knowlton, a lieutenant colonel with the Rangers—a volunteer group of elite intelligence officers—to investigate the British plans for advancement. Knowlton's Rangers realized the British soldiers were already headed north, so they led them into an ambush. While the Continental Army engaged the British Army from the front, the Rangers attacked them from the right to help deliver a swift victory. After this battle, the British Army retreated from a number of points north, making the Battle of Harlem Heights a strategic and morale-boosting victory for the Americans.

The British Army had brought their own elite forces to the Battle of Harlem Heights: the "42nd Highland Regiment of Foot" or the Black Watch, a Scottish infantry regiment formed by Jacobites, who were loyal to the Catholic King James II, after he had been deposed by William III in 1688. For decades the Jacobites rebelled against English rule over Scotland, and in 1715 they carried the motto of "No Hanover. No Union." Despite their doughtiness, they did not turn their discontent fully against the British as they engaged in conflicts around the world. Given their exceptional skills in battle, it is a bit of a mystery why they capitulated and continued to fight for England when they had misgivings about the validity of England's colonial ambitions.

The village of Manhattanville was founded on the site of the Battle of Harlem Heights in 1806. In 1811 a barrier gate called the Manhattanville Pass was set up at 123rd Street and Bloomingdale Road, which would become known as Broadway, to offer further protection from English aggression. When the New York state legislature developed the Commissioners' Plan of 1811 featuring twelve north-south avenues and 155 cross streets, Manhattanville was incorporated into the map of the new city.

●

Modern Manhattanville is thought to run along Broadway, from 123rd to 135th. It lies just north of Morningside Heights, known as the "beautiful hilltop" or the "Acropolis" because it is home to several internationally acclaimed cultural institutions. The university moved its campus from 49th Street and Madison Avenue to Morningside Heights in 1897, when it took over the campus of the Bloomingdale Insane Asylum. By the early 1900s, Barnard had also moved into Morningside Heights and found company with several soon to be notable institutions: St. Luke's Hospital, Union Theological Seminary, and Teachers College. The Cathedral of St. John the Divine was founded nearby in 1893 on the site of a former orphanage. At the Heights' highest point, Grant's Tomb was erected in the 1890s on a site that George Washington had once considered for the nation's capital. Next to the tomb is the Claremont Playground, built on the former site of the Claremont Inn founded in 1780, a vacation home to the upper classes. Presidents McKinley and Taft, the actress Lillian Russell, the songwriter Cole Porter, many Vanderbilts, Astors, and other well-known families could be seen taking a break from the hectic pace of downtown city life.

When my son was younger, we used to frequent the Claremont Playground, in the shadow of the Tomb's marble rotunda. I find Grant's Tomb to be a forlorn place, especially during the seasons when the trees lining the mall in front of it stand bare. My son, however, finds it fascinating because two bodies reside there, their coffins in plain view. Often he wants to visit when we pass by, but despite being a frequent stop for tour buses, the tomb is only open for one hour slots at time: 10:00–11:00 AM; 12:00–1:00 PM; 2:00–3:00 PM; and 4:00–5:00 PM, Wednesday through Sunday. The words Grant wrote to the 1868 Republican National Convention in his acceptance letter for the presidential nomination, "Let us have peace," are inscribed on a plaque between two female figures sitting over the entranceway of the tomb.

•

Manhattanville's development occurred around more mundane aspirations. Access to the Hudson and numerous natural waterways spurred industry, transforming the neighborhood into a transportation and manufacturing center for northern Manhattan. D. F. Tiemann & Co. Color Works, a pigment and dye factory owned by Daniel Tiemann, mayor of New York from 1858 to 1860, remained in business until around 1913. Breweries, milk bottlers, iron works, and storage facilities also boomed because of Manhattanville's proximity to the Hudson River.

Class disparity increased in Manhattanville after the Civil War. Many of the wealthy lived in excellent conditions while the poorest residents made dwellings out of whatever materials they could find. Some even built homes out of crates discarded by manufacturers in the area. Dogs, goats, cows, and pigs were raised in these shantytowns. The Sheltering Arms asylum cared for destitute children and a separate asylum for African American children was set up farther uptown. In 1876 Charles Loring Brace, founder of the Children's Aid Society, noted that many children in Harlem survived by hiding out in boxes, hay barges, and under stairwells through winter storms though barely and not without great suffering. The move to set up shelters for impoverished children coincided with a rise in moral expectations for the less fortunate across the city, though the desire to keep poverty and its consequences out of sight have always been part of that plan.

•

My son is connected to Manhattanville in a way I will never be, in part because he was born here, but also because he studies every building he passes. The other day, just before dinner, he told my husband that they were going on an adventure. My son led him out of our apartment, over to Broadway, then down 125th Street, up Old Broadway right to the threshold of the huge public housing projects, the Manhattanville Houses, and then right onto 126th Street through the doors of St. Mary's Protestant Episcopal Church. My husband, who has lived in the neighborhood for more than ten years, had never before entered this building. They sat quietly for ten minutes before filling out a visitor's card and returning home for dinner.

Since 1823 St. Mary's had welcomed the wealthy, though many members were quite poor. In recognition of this fact, Reverend William Richmond ceased the practice of charging worshippers to rent pews in 1831, making St. Mary's the first free Episcopal church in the US. Congregants included white landowners as well as African American business owners in the village, and the church also started the city's first free, mixed-race school a few blocks to the south, near to the spot where Manhattanville's other public housing development, the General Ulysses S. Grant Houses, now stands.

Manhattanville maintained a majority of American-born white people even as it became attractive to recent immigrants from all over Europe. African Americans had lived in Harlem since the seventeenth-century Dutch colonial period, but after World War I, as part of the Great Migration nearly 200,000 Black southerners moved here in search of jobs in factories and slaughterhouses. At the same time, greater Harlem welcomed large numbers of Jewish immigrants, refugees from Eastern Europe, who had fled the dilapidated low-rises of the Lower East Side for the wide streets and hills of Uptown. Visible reminders of this integration remain in the synagogue on Old Broadway to the Church of the Annunciation on 131st, completed and dedicated in 1854, the first Catholic church to be built above 2nd Street on the West Side. The ambitions of all these newcomers fueled the area's industrial growth.

•

Most of the old industrial buildings in the corridor have been razed, and scaffolding for one of the largest university buildings is going up, though it is difficult to make out its final shape. From the signs posted around the worksite it is clear that this new campus will be above us all, with floating windows affixed to steel armature. Later, when I look at images of the proposed structures on the university's website, I see figures inside, silhouettes in a world that appears, in these renderings, to be superimposed and imaginary.

•

The Great Depression brought significant changes to the quality of life in Manhattanville, which for all intents and purposes had been absorbed by then into Greater Harlem. Those who could afford to leave moved to the suburbs as joblessness and crime rose in Uptown neighborhoods. In 1934 just a few weeks after his inauguration, Mayor Fiorello La Guardia created legislation for the first municipal housing authority in America. He wanted to eliminate the city's slums, which he believed to be the breeding grounds for social disorders.

Architect and developer Fred F. French preceded La Guardia in thinking that a large, self-contained enclave could be instrumental in bringing a community back into prosperity. In 1928 he invested in poor properties in the East Forties, then demolished them to erect Tudor City, one of the country's first affordable housing developments. Touted as "a city within a city," each of the eleven buildings was designed to help residents disregard the slaughterhouses that surrounded them. This impulse to replace declining neighborhoods with new ones was supported by the US Housing Act of 1937, which provided financial assistance to cities. The federal government paid for the debt on these high-rises, and subsidies were given to owners and managers of public housing so that rents might be reduced.

The US Housing Act of 1949 made provisions for suitable living conditions for every American family. In effect it gave municipalities federal subsidies to cover up to two-thirds of the costs of acquiring land, relocating tenants, razing existing structures, and reselling land to private developers. Expenses associated with new construction—roads, schools, streetlights, and sewers—comprised the remaining one-third of funding. New York State paid for one-half of these costs, which meant the city was only responsible for only one-sixth. Often construction was privately financed through separate funds.

•

One strategy for dealing with poverty is to change the conditions that make it possible. Another way is to relocate the poor, so those responsible for creating disparity do not have to face the consequences of it. There are nobler ideas that fall somewhere between these extremes, as the issue is not easy to solve. Maybe the problem is assuming that a space belongs to people in time: a class, race, or ethnicity. The truth is that space belongs to no one. More likely we belong to all of the streets that brought us here. These places are threaded together by our shared history, our habit of living in the wrong place at the wrong time, of dragging ourselves from one edge of ruin to the next.

I remember myself in locations that no longer exist, and this is how I am able to believe that, at some point, I was free.

African Americans from Southern states and Puerto Ricans became more prominent residents of Manhattanville by the 1950s, and many settled on Claremont Avenue after World War II. Met with suspicion, these new residents struggled to integrate the area's flagging business interests. Tiemann's color factory closed in 1913. In 1951 the Claremont Inn burned to the ground in a fire during demolition, and the neighborhood fell into disrepair. Around this time master city planner and societal engineer Robert Moses partnered with philanthropist David Rockefeller, who had grown up in the neighborhood, to develop Morningside Gardens, a middle-class, mixed-race, cooperative housing project, in order to stabilize the residential community. Morningside Gardens was built with an eye to modernism and with the support of all the major institutions on the hill above it— Riverside Church, International House, Barnard College, Columbia University, Corpus Christi Church, the Jewish Theological Seminary, the Juilliard School of Music, Teachers College, and Union Theological Seminary—as it displaced poorer residents and demolished tenements. Critics argued that the compound was designed as a buffer to keep black and Puerto Rican populations from moving southward.

Just to the north of Morningside Gardens, which opened in 1957, Moses had also pushed for the development of two large low-income housing developments, the General Grant Houses and the Manhattanville Houses.

•

Longstanding rivalries are not uncommon amongst neighboring public housing complexes throughout New York City. Out in the Rockaways, recurring conflicts amongst residents of Beach 41st Street Houses, Ocean Bay Houses, and Ocean Village have erupted. More than 4,500 people live in the nine buildings that make up the Grant Houses, the larger of the neighborhood's city-run developments. Just across 125th St. on the north side, sits the Manhattanville Houses, comprised of six buildings and more than 2,500 people. Some of the shops that fall on the north side of 125th Street are regarded as Manhattanville Houses territory, just as some of the shops that fall on the south side of the street are seen as "belonging" to those who live in the Grant Houses.

No one has been able to point a finger at the original source of conflict between these two developments, but initial fights over pride, romantic relationships, or boasting might have been resolved by a fistfight. The widespread availability of guns have made the conflicts more likely to escalate, despite the fact that gun violence is harder for the police to ignore than other kinds of assaults. Since the murder of Tayshana Murphy, a beloved high school senior and nationally ranked point guard in September of 2011, some fifty shooting incidents including nineteen non-fatal shootings and have been reported in the vicinity. In early June of 2014, four people were injured by pellets from BB guns in separate incidents near the university's satellite employment office on Broadway and 125th Street.

Fights in the streets and at nearby restaurants continued to flare up even after Murphy's accused killers were
arrested in South Carolina, ten days after the murder. In
October of that same year, a boy was shot at Amsterdam
and West 129th Street. In May of the following spring, a
twenty-four-year-old man was shot in the stomach at the
Grant Houses early in the afternoon. I read local blogs to
keep informed of incidents like these, because they are
underreported in the mainstream media.

Most of the time, Manhattanville moves easily in its rou-
tines: people head to work, to school. The streets are
generally not sites of public recklessness or drunken
altercations. Who knows what goes on in private
homes, but on Broadway even teenagers seem to avoid
stunts and antics that one might see in wealthier neighborhoods. Restraint manifests in those of us who quietly wait for the M104 bus. Perhaps this composure is a
result of caution, fatigue, or the need to disengage with
our rapidly changing surroundings.

In times when I am particularly awake on the street,
I have the feeling there is unfinished business, some
anxiety over a struggle that predates the arrival of
the Grant and Manhattanville Houses. I can't help but
think back to the Battle of Harlem Heights, when two
elite forces engaged each other thanks to the provoca-

tions of a monarchy. Here in the decrescendo of summer, the Rangers fought Scotland's Black Watch across
the Hollow Way—which became Manhattan Street and
then 125th Street—for control of the territory, the very
same land on which the two housing developments
now stand.

Both regiments encountered bad fortune: Knowlton
and the commander of the Black Watch died during
this battle. Following the war, the Scottish regiments
were never formally recognized for their service—as
the British Army offered no benefits for defending the
King's interests within the Anglosphere—thus com-
pounding the loss of life and freedom.

These days it is the university that seems to be winning
the territory of Manhattanville.

•

When the Manhattanville Houses were completed in
1961, more attention was paid to their landscaping
than to architectural features inside the buildings and
individual apartments. This focus on landscape design
presented a facade of environmental concern for its
residents. But by 1986 the North River Water Pollution
Control Plant had been opened at 137th to 145th Streets

after after having been pushed north from its originally planned site at 72nd Street, despite protests from
Uptown residents. Riverbank Park was placed on top of
the facility to ameliorate residents' initial distrust of its
negative environmental impact, the least of which was
a persistent smell of rotten eggs. Action by the West
Harlem Environmental Action Committee forced a solution for the odor, but diminished air quality continues
to be a problem. The plant has created complications
along Harlem's waterfront as well. When an explosion
and fire allowed wastewater to be released into the
Hudson in July 2011, few remembered the activists who
had warned about accidental outcomes such as this.

By the time the Harlem Fairway grocery store
opened between the Riverside Drive Viaduct and the
defunct Harlem Piers in 1995, Manhattanville had long
been home to taxi dispatches, bus depots, gas stations,
self-storage centers, and meatpackers. In addition to
the sewage treatment center and marine garbage collection transfer station, Amtrak's diesel-driven Adirondack
trains pass through the area on their way to Albany. To
the east, the No. 1 subway train bolts from underground
north at 120th Street and thunders over the Manhattan
Viaduct. Planes on a flight path to and from LaGuardia
Airport are a constant presence. Morning and afternoon
commuter congestion on the Henry Hudson Parkway,

combined with pollution from three-quarters of the city's diesel bus depots, further compromises the air of this once bucolic valley. Add to the mess the exhaust from large trucks hauling HVAC systems for new sky-scrapers, boats, or modular houses, which can enter the city via Broadway. Just before Thanksgiving we watched a flatbed haul the Norway spruce that would become the Christmas tree at Rockefeller Center. It is no won-der hospitalization rates for asthma are twenty-one times higher here than in Manhattan's least-affected neighborhoods.

I worry about air quality while my son interprets this traffic as evidence that we reside at the center of the world. Any change in its flow is a cause for celebra-tion and questions. During a recent rainstorm, planes approaching LaGuardia Airport shifted their flight path and created a stream of engines and lights shooting low over Manhattanville about every two minutes. My son had already been in bed a half-hour when he called me to look outside. The planes were close enough that he could read their logos. *Look, Mom,* he said. *Delta!* And then *Look, Mom. Southwest!* My husband was in the bedroom fold-ing the whites. *I see the American Airlines plane!* After five more jets passed, I told him he needed to go to sleep, but when I left his room I stood at the kitchen window watch-ing the planes, too. I could not deny flight is the antidote to doubt of all kinds. I kept my eyes on the sky like my son, who I knew was still standing at his window.

•

It is funny how quickly one can feel a sense of ownership and entitlement when living in a neighborhood. These days I say Manhattanville is my home, but I am a transplant. My husband lived here when I met him, and, once we were engaged, I broke the lease on my Brooklyn apartment to move in with him. Proximity to the university brought my husband to rent a room here in the early aughts, but wider gentrification began with black professionals moving back to Harlem in the 1990s. Some chose Uptown out of a desire to experience pleasant exchanges with their neighbors, instead of being treated like an interloper, as they had felt in other upper middle-class areas of the city. At that time Manhattanville, zoned as Manhattan Community District 9 (Manhattanville, Hamilton Heights, and Morningside Heights), was 39.1% black, 36.1% Latino, 19.5% white, and 4.5% Asian. Harlem's housing stock also afforded new residents larger apartments than could be found in most of Manhattan. In the current moment, most of Harlem's prosperity is concentrated east of Manhattanville, just past Morningside Park. Restaurants featuring celebrity chefs, luxury apartments, a Whole Foods, and other chain retailers are obvious markers. With the rise of the new university buildings, however, new restaurants catering to wealthy student tastes have become more prominent in the area.

Though the university answered protests against the new campus with a promise of jobs and cultural opportunity, the dynamics of Manhattanville's social relations are complicated by university students, both graduate and undergraduate, who do not live here long enough to commit to the neighborhood. Their arrival in fall causes the most noticeable disruption, when these newbies, nervous about being in the city, travel in loud packs that hesitate to yield to oncoming pedestrians. In early evenings, young women feign confidence as they stagger to the train in fashionable heels. At the end of the night, intoxicated with the city, they stumble back up the street, barefoot. Music students sing operatically at the stop, as if they are the first to discover the subway platform as stage. By snowfall, most of these performances cease, as these temporary residents wise up to the pitfalls of being conspicuously dramatic.

Longtime Manhattanville residents form the front-row audience, a silent, incandescent amphitheater— from the grand tenements at the west to the two public housing projects at the east to the cooperatively owned Morningside Gardens at the south.

•

To the casual observer, the towers of the Grant and
Manhattanville public housing projects to the north and
those of the Morningside Gardens cooperative community to the south the superblocks on either side of La
Salle Street near Broadway might look like one large
community instead of two. But closer study reveals
distinct differences in design. The Manhattanville and
Grant Houses are both ombre brick towers with narrow
double-hung windows. The Morningside Gardens apartments feature triple-hung windows, which let more light
inside the apartments. This minor innovation reflected
the trends or modern architects such as György Kepes
and Mies van der Rohe, who believed glass gave a
building a sense of transparency, reflection, and open-
ness. The residences at Morningside Gardens also feature balconies, green spaces with seasonal landscaping
around entrances, private security guards, playrooms,
workout centers, and party rooms, as well as a private
preschool.

My son attended that preschool for three years
when I was feeling most vulnerable about my work/fam-
ily life balance, which is to say I experienced only imbal-
ance. I rushed from my office in the Village to meet him
by 5:30 p.m. pickup, feeling just as guilty as I did when I

dropped him off in the morning. Walking home together was the highlight of my day, even though he would often be cranky and slow on foot.

On the afternoon of June 8, 2012, three men were shot at point-blank range as they waited in a parked BMW on West 122nd Street near Broadway. The killer discarded a shirt he had used to wipe away his fingerprints in a trash bin at La Salle and Broadway just around the time that my son and I passed by. The bodies were not discovered until about a half hour later, which I learned that evening when my husband received an alert from the university's emergency notification system.

I know that violence is change that occurs too quickly. No conflict is ever solved because of it—only suppressed. But violence makes even less sense when it weakens a community's ability to respond to powerful interests that are reshaping its relationship to place. Some days I think about this when I walk between the Grant Houses and Morningside Gardens. Other days I think about my grocery list and deadlines.

When all around me the big pieces keep moving, I have trouble knowing if what I see is real. Am I a part of this place or just an observer? Do I play a role in its history, or will I fail to leave any significant mark? Most likely the latter is true, though my ego makes me want to believe otherwise. Every day I take the train from my office, get off at the station nearest to my apartment. I pick up my son, and together we make our way home.

We are traffic.

•

During rush hour a train moving in either direction arrives on the Manhattan Viaduct at 125th Street every three minutes or so, each one sounding a bit like a plane landing on Broadway. The number 1 line features the R62A subway cars, built between 1984 and 1987 by Bombardier in La Pocatière, Québec, a town situated on the south shore of the St. Lawrence. These cars are completed in Barre, Vermont, under a license from Kawasaki. Between jackhammers on the street, sand-blasters cleaning the stone on the subway riser, and the brake problems on the R62As, especially the weekend cars, I feel as though I am always at attention, a sentry for the small platoon that is my family. Still I prefer this thunder to the sound of its absence, which happens occasionally during storms and for at least twenty-four hours during Hurricane Sandy. That quiet, in many ways, felt more foreboding, as if it was now clear to the world that we all had somehow failed each other.

•

One morning after a snowstorm, my husband and I walked to the gym, past the Blue Flame, a gas and restaurant-supply shop, where in 2009, four men were shot by the owner during an attempted robbery. Two of the men died. Because I was feeling confident in my understanding of history, I spoke out loud about how surprised I was to see the store was still open. I read the handwritten sign above the door: *Abandon all hope, ye who enter here.* I thought, Dante, *The Inferno,* when a man in a blue work shirt said to us, *I was there.* He told us about seeing the thieves outside the shop a few minutes, *Before they barged in and put a gun to my temple.* He spoke with us for nearly a half hour about the ordeal. By the time we parted my head was so full that when I arrived at the gym I spent my time there transcribing the conversation. A few weeks later, I accidentally threw the notes into a garbage bag of papers I planned on discarding when I cleaned my desk. Deep down I did not want to recall everything the man said because the vision of the future of the neighborhood he offered was cataclysmic, a violent apocalypse.

The first building on the university's new campus is nearly finished. Soon there will be real persons drifting behind the shimmering glass. To outsiders the evolution of a neighborhood will seem transparent.

Once you know a place well, it is impossible not to feel impacted by the history that shaped it: the unresolved conflicts, debts, lasting grudges, smokestack grime, lost children, unwelcomed newcomers, busted doors, broken agreements, misdelivered mercies, dishonored sacrifices, nostalgia for segregation, those who wander without a sense of direction, the besotted, the vanquished, and dispossessed.

And though I know these stories and have, at times, lived in the midst of them, they are both mine and not mine, though facts can sound like my truth in the moment I speak them.

In the dark early morning of June 4, 2014, three years after the murder of Tayshana Murphy, five hundred NYPD officers arrived before daybreak at the Manhattanville and General Grant Houses to perform a highly choreographed raid. My husband and son were awakened by low-flying helicopters that flashed spotlights into apartments and up and down the narrow alleys between buildings. Residents as far over as Lenox Avenue were disturbed from sleep. By dawn, one hundred and three people had been arrested. Police Commissioner William Bratton confirmed the conflicts did not arise over drugs or money, but from disputes over territory in and around the housing projects.

According to the eighty-six-count indictment filed by Manhattan district attorney Cyrus Vance, young people from Manhattanville and Grant Houses participated in seventy shooting incidents, including two murders, over the previous four years. The 168-page document was posted online immediately following the arrests. Many of the Overt Acts related to conspiracy charges were committed on social media, primarily on Facebook, where the accused allegedly sought to buy firearms, threatened residents of the neighboring houses, and stated aspirations for revenge.

Following the raid, a quiet sense of dread filled the air as neighbors whispered about the young people, mostly men, who had been suddenly removed, dislocated, and banished. Critics of the raid included some who were displeased with the police department's military tactics. Others wondered about the legitimacy of a case that implicated so many people. Residents of the Grant and Manhattanville Houses who had asked for help from the police before Murphy was murdered made it clear that basic precautions, such as fixing the locks on exterior doors, might have helped to calm the trouble.

In summer, just a few weeks later, a sudden rise in gang recruitment activity in the housing projects was reported by a local blogger. Children between the ages of ten and fourteen were amongst the most eager to join the crews. By October representatives from both developments gathered in meetings held by the West Harlem Development Corporation to discuss the upcoming court cases and opportunities for peaceful reconciliation. Because we all were still in shock over the arrests, it was too soon to predict the success of any of these efforts.

Opinions on the future of the neighborhood remain divided, as it is still a place where one may walk without recognition of change or history.

When the Sea Comes for Us

And you, oh ye great little fish! ye tadpoles, ye sprats, ye minnows, ye chubbs, ye grubs, ye barnacles, and all you small fry of literature, be cautious how you insult my new launched vessel, or swim within my view; lest in a moment of mingled sportiveness and scorn, I sweep you up in a scoop net, and roast a half hundred of you for breakfast.
—Diedrich Knickerbocker a.k.a. Washington Irving,
A History of New York

Wherein differ the sea and the land, that a miracle upon one is not a miracle upon the other?
—Herman Melville, *Moby-Dick*

I OFFER THIS INVOCATION as an act of optimism and faith in our ability to ride the change. After Hurricane Sandy flooded the tunnels and shorelines of Manhattan in the fall of 2012, the bottom half of the city slipped into a darkness more complete than the blackout of 1977, and we had no choice but to ponder the likelihood of future breaches of the island by wind and sea.

The ocean surrounding us is formless, immense, mercurial, and subject to forces we do not entirely understand. It does not relent in its vastness or unpredictability, and its blue lulls us into believing we have witnessed infinity.

A true sea change will leave no territory unaffected. To find our place in this rising water, our best bet might be to board a boat like Verazano did and discover America again.

·

Waves in the ocean are composed of crests and troughs. The crest, or the apex of a wave, is its highest point; the trough functions as the inverse. The structural components of the wave move in inconsistent ways, as they are subject to tides that move according to the gravitational pulls of the moon, and the Earth's own rotation. Waves work as units of change and transformation; thus we arrive at one place just as it becomes another.

By luck or good fortune, we are drawn to this shore. Perhaps it is the Hudson Canyon, an ancient riverbed nearly twice as deep as the Grand Canyon, that pulls us in. From here we sail northward toward a verdant archipelago. We follow the tide from the Lower Bay, which sits between Rockaway, Queens, on Long Island and Sandy Hook in New Jersey, up through the Narrows, where since 1964 the Verrazano-Narrows Bridge connects the boroughs of Staten Island and Brooklyn, to finally arrive at the body of water known as the Upper Bay.

•

After a hundred leagues we found a very agreeable place between two small but prominent hills; between them a very wide river, deep at its mouth, flow out into the sea; and with the help of the tide, which rises eight feet, any laden ship could have passed from the sea into the river estuary.[1]

—Giovanni da Verrazano

Despite its calm appearance, the Upper Bay is a site of significant movement and volatility. Approximately twelve billion cubic feet of water per tide flows from it into the Lower Bay through the Narrows. These waters constantly mix with the outflow of the Hudson River. In 1524, as Verrazano made his course to the Upper Bay, it teemed with marine life.

The water appears impervious to our ambitions— our best and our worst. But we also misinterpret its power following storms as a kind of acquiescence to trouble. Maybe this means we have mistaken water for the messenger instead of the message. And what would it mean to be lost to the water?

•

After studying Verrazano's writings, Henry Hudson, the famed English explorer, came upon New York's Upper Bay in 1609 in search of a route across North America to the Pacific Ocean. He called New York's remote and lonely harbor a "haven where a thousand ships may ride in safety."

During a second trip to North America in 1611, Hudson's ship, Discovery, entered the top of Hudson Bay at the outset of an Arctic winter with the hope of reaching Asia. His crew mutinied when they suspected Hudson had been hoarding food. He and several others were put onto a small boat and sent afloat. They were never heard from again.

•

Let's imagine that from our schooner we can see the shark-finned edge of lower Manhattan in 1650, when its shoreline was first extended into the Hudson and East Rivers.

Further expansions of the Battery into the Hudson followed in 1800, 1965, and 1980, when three million

cubic yards of soil and rock excavated during the construction of the World Trade Center towers created
Battery Park City, a development of posh apartments
facing the tidal estuary of the Hudson River. Engineering
the shore continued the tradition of leveling Manhattan
by filling ponds, mudflats, streams and wetlands.

Building upward had something to do with the economy
of space, but one would be remiss in ignoring the thrill
of vertical architecture. Consider the Empire State
Building, which rose to its height of 103 stories in just
a little over a year, nearly four and a half feet per week,
or 1,250 feet in all. The impulse to climb may also have
been the result of a desire to separate the wealthy from
the poor, an attempt to ascend to great heights. Some
argue that the first families of industry—the Fultons,
Astors, Rockefellers, Vanderbilts, and other big fish who
became the financial leaders of the city, and patrons to
causes they felt just—erected monuments to match
their own self-estimations. It is overstatement to say
they built the skyline, as other laborers did the work,
but the confidence of these magnates spurred architects
and engineers to stack the city so that all occupants of
these towers might have a chance to gain perspective
on the dynamic between the city and the sea. It should
not be surprising, then, that the high-rise owes its name

to seafaring, as *skyscraper* originally defined the sail on the tallest mast of a ship, which from deck appeared to be raking through the sky.

•

How effective these towers have been in keeping us from studying the water, from cataloguing its vibrant marine life. We missed seeing shellfish beds so large that they exceeded the city itself in size. In 1887 the Fulton Fish Market sold 50,000 oysters per day. Blackfish, striped bass, and drum filled the bay, flinting and slipping away in explosions of silver and gold. In 1916 four men caught 120 croakers during a four-hour period. In 1932 mackerel overtook the harbor as schools of slick instinct, but they could not outrun the impurities brought by the city's combined storm water and sewage systems.

In the early 1940s, one habitual pilgrim to the water's edge profiled local cultures dependent on the sea while bringing attention to the harbor's appalling contamination:

> The bulk of the water in New York Harbor is oily, dirty, and germy. Men on the mud suckers, the big harbor dredges, like to say that you could bottle it and sell it for poison.
> —Joseph Mitchell, "The Bottom of the Harbor"

After centuries of using the harbor as dump, the water turned toxic. By 1910 oysters were making people ill; some say they even brought about an epidemic of typhoid fever. Despite those suspicions, in 1912 a small group of scientists developed a formula to support the claim that the harbor could accommodate the sewage of sixty million people. Any algorithm that advocates for more pollution is suspect, but even if it was optimistic, at best, evidence that marine life in the harbor was suffering continued to mount.

Pollution had been a concern before 1903, when the New York Bay Commission was founded by the state. In 1906 the state legislature passed a law allowing for the creation of the Metropolitan Sewerage Committee, which encouraged broader investigation of pollution by the city. Out of concern for sea life, scientists tracked waning levels of dissolved oxygen at the beginning of the twentieth century. Lowered levels of dissolved oxygen in the water meant stress on wildlife, resulting in "gas bubble disease" or widespread die-offs. The bay was drowning in garbage.

While sewage disposal into the harbor has subsided, four treatment plants still pour more than 250 million gallons of wastewater into the bay. And even though some of the plants have been recently renovated to reduce their output of nitrogen, polluted rainwater and sewage overflows remain variables. Following

Hurricane Sandy, ten of the city's fourteen wastewater treatment plants sustained damage, and predictions of damage from future storms remain dire.

•

Despite these environmental challenges, conditions for sea life in New York Harbor continue to improve. Scientists have been cultivating oyster beds, once nearly extinct, to help in removing algae and excess nitrogen from polluted waters. This low-tech solution, combined with upgrades in wastewater management, meant that in 2012 New York Harbor was cleaner than it had been in one hundred years. In the past three years, dozens of harbor seals and whales have been spotted. No one knows if their return is a result of improved water quality, warmer temperatures, or a migrating food supply. Or perhaps these species have come to warn us that deeper waters are soon to be on the way.

The truth is that we don't know where we are going amidst the volume. When one feels adrift, an onboard journey appears to progress in fits and starts. In an attempt to reclaim our confidence we circle the harbor and catch sight of a humpback breaching, Brooklyn in the background. Gentle waves slap at the bulkhead. Soft humid air makes it pleasant to breathe deeply. The Statue of Liberty is turned toward the open sea, as if in recognition of the fact that hope arrives from someplace else. Tourists flock to the bottom of Manhattan to witness the myth of a limitless America in towers of glass that mirror the sky. Here comes the Staten Island Ferry crossing the five miles from St. George Terminal to Whitehall Street more than one hundred times a day.

•

> *O Captain! my Captain! our fearful trip is done, / The ship has weather'd every rack, the prize we sought is won, / The port is near, the bells I hear, the people all exulting, / While follow eyes the steady keel, the vessel grim and daring. . .*
>
> —Walt Whitman, "O Captain! My Captain!"

The sea serves as metaphor for what we cannot understand. It has been a bridge between nations, the chasm between freedom and slavery, a cemetery for the lost, a home to riches. It has been our adversary and only friend. It is older and bigger than us, and it changes all we know about time and distance.

•

Now small fowls flew screaming over the yet yawning gulf;
a sullen white surf beat against its steep sides; then all col-
lapsed, and the great shroud of the sea rolled on as it rolled
five thousand years ago.

—Herman Melville, *Moby-Dick*

In July of 2010, during the construction for the new World Trade Center, a brigantine was discovered in the landfill that supported the Hudson River bulkhead between Liberty and Cedar Streets. The two-masted vessel is believed to have been a Hudson River sloop built in Philadelphia around 1773 then discarded around 1810. The boat measured sixty to seventy feet long and eighteen feet wide. The discovery of teredos in its frame, a kind of shipworm native to the South Atlantic, suggests it was used to bring food, wood, and livestock to and from the Caribbean. Otherwise the ship was found to be in excellent condition as its position in the landfill kept it from being exposed to the elements.

Another merchant ship was found in 1982 when crews constructed a tower near the South Street Seaport development. This vessel had also been discarded during the mid-1800s. And in 1916, during the foundational work on the 7th Avenue Line of the New York City Subway system, workers discovered a boat eighteen feet below what was then the intersection of Greenwich and Dey Streets. Remains of several other vessels reside in Coney Island Creek in southern Brooklyn, and a number of shipwrecks can be found where the Hudson River enters the bay.

These relics cast an eerie premonition as they point to the most vulnerable flood zones of the city, as if they are not ruins but, rather, an armada for the future, one poised to set sail when the sea reclaims Manhattan.

So why not sink our schooner here in brackish waters? Let it rest in the silt, until it is called back to sail.

•

When we go ashore we learn the island has been cut by freshwater, too. Ancient underground streams, or watercourses, flow through bedrock and beneath buildings.

Egbert Ludovicus Viele's "Water Map" of 1874 indicates the locations of the city's natural springs, marshes, and meadowlands and still proves to be key to the success of construction projects in the city. Though Viele completed his hydrology map after much of Manhattan's topography had been altered, it has proven to be one of the best indicators for how likely a given location might be prone to erosion. His map divides Manhattan into colors: saturated greens point to creeks and wetlands;

blues depict shorelines. The fabricated shores of the Battery and much of Lower Manhattan are peach, making the island, for a moment, appear like a flower, its shoreline as petals reaching outward.

Many of the watercourses Viele noted continue to exist, despite substantial buildings constructed over them. Minetta Brook, the fabled ancient stream around which Manhattan first became a city, is said to surface at the entryway of an apartment building at Two 5th Avenue.[2] The likelihood that this stream still runs is unlikely, as in 1930 it was rumored to have dried up.[3] Near St. Nicholas Park and 141st Street, a few of the brownstones have been known to have "wet basements," meaning a stream flows beneath the subflooring.

An active watercourse moves through the lower level of Prentis Hall, a Columbia University building at 125th Street near 10th Avenue, which once operated as a milk factory. A trough was dug to channel the flow through the building out into a sewer on 125th Street. We hear it babble as we enter the basement. According to Viele's map, Prentis sits at the junction between two separate streams: Indian Spring and Tiemann Fountain. Outside, the streets appear undisturbed and motionless.

●

Among the numerous events, which are each in their turn the most direful and melancholy of all possible occurrences, in your interesting and authentic history; there is none that occasions such heart rending grief to your historian of sensibility, as the decline and fall of your renowned and mighty empires!
—Diedrich Knickerbocker a.k.a. Washington Irving,
A History of New York

A ship is a vehicle for romance, or at the very least, cooperation. It serves as its own universe once it sets sail, and makes it possible for one to endure not just the sea but the experience of solitude and disconnection. *To ship* is to bring an idea or object across a distance. It is also the gesture of sending something away.

When Hurricane Sandy made landfall in October of 2012, thousands of buildings believed to be outside the flood zone were impacted. This was, in part, due to the use of outdated flood maps from the Federal Emergency Management Agency (FEMA), which were well-studied in the hours leading up to the storm. When the maps were revised in 2014, nearly 35,000 buildings were recognized to be at risk, for the first time.

Some of the mitigation plans under consideration include building a floodgate in the harbor; retrofitting existing buildings and equipping them with elevated entrances in the case of high water; designating flood zones in the lowest lying areas of the island; raising flood-walls and bulkheads; and developing parks in the areas most vulnerable to flooding. In June 2014, 148 architects and engineers submitted designs for flood mitigation programs to the U.S. Department of Housing and Urban Development. $920 million in grants will be split amongst the ten winning proposals, though skeptics argue that these plans severely underestimate the pace of climate change and will only provide short-term relief. Others argue these initiatives will give us time to develop better long-term solutions.

We do know that when the sea comes for us, we won't be trapped on the third floor of our apartment building for weeks without heat or electricity as the lobby takes on four feet of water. We won't worry as asphalt roads ribbon under the pressure of tides, disintegrating to rock and then gravel. We won't shudder at the sound of a transformer exploding like a bomb in the night after some unknown surge. We won't turn our faces away from fires that leap from rooftop to rooftop but cannot be extinguished by the brine surrounding them. We won't be stunned to see the rail channels of the renovated South Ferry Terminal flood with water and garbage. We won't ache as one-hundred-year-old trees are pulled from the soil by the rising current. We won't watch houses topple after floating a half-mile down the street. We won't gasp in disbelief when a 168-foot water tanker breaks free from its moorings and hurtles toward what's left of the shore. We won't because we will have raised our ship from the muck and steered it toward the next landing that will become New York, no matter what that place is called when we find it.

Notes

1. *The Written Record of the Voyage of 1524 of Giovanni da Verrazano as recorded in a letter to Francis I, King of France, July 8th, 1524.* www.columbia.edu/~lmg21/ash3002y/earlyac99/documents/verrazan.htm.

2. From the plaque in the lobby:

> A brook winds its erratic way beneath this site
> The Indians called it Manette or Devil's Water
> To the Dutch settlers it was
> Bestevaer's Killetje or Grandfather's Little Creek
> For the past two centuries familiar to this neighbor-
> hood as
> Minetta Brook

3. http://watercourses.typepad.com/.a/6a00e55019a4e988340105349e2778970c-popup

Norway

WHEN I AND WHOEVER else was left of Black America finally got out of there, we met up in Norway. The war had taken years off our memory of each other. We had not integrated enough technology into our rituals of self-absorption to say for certain when we completely lost sight of the future. We had no unnatural access to the past, and what little we knew about our home was found only in the library.

Most of us arrived before the fourth of July, just in time for the eve of Sankt Hans, and the long, white nights of midsummer. We did not know then how many children would be born the following March, but our passion did not surprise the Norwegians who were already used to a fecund spring season. The ambassadors Voltemand and Cornelius greeted us with the customary gentleness we came to expect.

Single black women were encouraged to sleep with seven kinds of wildflowers pressed under their pillows in order to help them dream of the right man to marry, if they preferred a man. The custom, though regional, seemed to make sense to us in an oddly personal way, though our traditions had been forged thousands of miles from here in a climate too humid to tolerate sleep during the summer.

Illegal immigrants of the Norwegian underklasse, who had been cast out to make room for us, had been targeted by the government for stealing education. One euphemism we used for them was *excess* or *overskytende*, a word we could not pronounce easily. We called them "skytenders" instead, which made them sound a bit like the oppressors during slavery. This helped us to think we were better than them as we claimed their neighborhoods for our neighborhoods.

Courses in Norwegian were offered by the Bergen Offentlige Bibliotek, which welcomed us with a tour of the building. As the library had been situated atop the former site of a brewery, we did not see any contradiction between studying language and enjoying a local pilsner or two.

Having little experience in navigating fjords, we traded our skills in mathematics for lessons on how to sail the inlets through the fog and silence. We brushed up on alienation and deadpan, too.

Those of us who could not speak Norwegian, Russian, or Greek took jobs in the tourist markets of Bergen. Those fluent in Swedish experienced the occasional disappointment of being mistaken for African. Some Africans wanted nothing to do with us after our exile from our second continent.

Three newspapers reported independently that the Black American had retained few competencies during the latest migration, but we garnered new ambitions faster than anyone expected, especially in the rail and fishing industries. Within months of our arrival, vestiges of the culture we had held on to for hundreds of years started to slip away into religion or mythology. The absence of history made the ones who had been the poorest indistinguishable from those who had been well-off.

Those most used to riding trains took over running the Norwegian State Railways (NSB). All season we delayed the evening departures out of kindness for tourists who rushed to catch the last trip out of town. Our night rides received top ratings in the *Lonely Planet* travel guide and one other tour book for English speakers in Scandinavia.

After two seasons of integration, it became harder to tell whom we belonged to and who belonged to us. When a sightseeing train arrived at the waterfall just before reaching Flåm, a man stood naked facing the water, his back to all those just arrived. When we called out to him, our tongues stung from salt in the air. Was he one or the other? When we called out to him, he did not turn, but that may not have been his answer.

Once the laws promoting citizenship were revoked following hysteria about the murder of several young skinheads, another migration commenced in the general direction of Iceland though not necessarily that far. It turned out that only a few of the murdered men were neo-Nazis, but because the purported assassin was suspected to be Negro, we were condemned as a group. *This is not a problem*, we emphasized even where our overcrowding in neighborhoods seemed to incite the most fear.

Trains running at high speeds often skipped a stop. Which ones they missed, though not easy to predict, were noted on the board as "Harlem," "St. Louis," or "Detroit" for reasons we would eventually understand as gestures of friendship.

By the time we earned control over the cod and salmon farming industries, outcry amongst the Norwegians was muted by a desire to maintain business ties with us. Our preparation of bacalao was demanded by international grocers for its authentic flavor, as was our smoked salmon, which came to be known as "Blackfisk" amongst the best restaurateurs.

Of course there would have been no need to go to Norway if we had had anywhere else to go. It wasn't fair that the land given to us belonged to someone else, but an international urgency to make recompense for egregious misdeeds perpetrated over centuries won over the standing values. The only thing to do was reckon with the present because the past bore costs that could never be added up. More brutality than could ever be accounted for. More stupidity than could ever be forgotten. More cruelty than could ever be enjoyed.

When it rained, we ate flatbread and lutefisk at the tourist cafés and reminisced about Mississippi, Jamaica, and Brazil. We listened to stories about how cold it felt before the oil was found and how the churches were the center of all hope, one island town after another. We confessed how quietly we had been chased out of the worst cities in America, and how we were glad to be free of the hope it could be anyway else.

About a year after we first arrived, the statue of Edvard Grieg in the Festplassen, in front of the Rikstelefon in Bergen, was stolen. A note left in its place said in English, *Yeah, we took him. He's ours now.*

The police searched the Fyllingsdalen neighborhood door to door but there was no sign of Grieg's statue. The conservatory committed to performing one of his sonatas each week until it was recovered. After a year the students grew frustrated with the lack of electronic instruments and became less willing to participate in the concerts. *Grieg is dead!* one young woman shouted before she was expelled from the concert hall. Despite the turmoil, we had become the most regular attendees at the free concerts, though most of us preferred his compositions from *Peer Gynt* and after.

In late summer, we swam in the mountain lakes atop Ulriken, at the edge of Bergen. It took us the whole day to hike that far. Below, the city looked big enough to welcome all travelers. Most of the ice had melted, and as we entered the water tiny frogs darted around us.

Norwegian fishermen were invited to move into the mountains above Ålesund and other port cities and make their living harvesting wild herbs and roots. When mixed with alcohol in a tincture, these remedies helped us to relax after a long day of hard work.

Acknowledgments

THANKS TO:

The editors of the following publications in which previous versions of these works appeared: *Harper's Magazine, The Iowa Review, Fence, Seneca Review, Everyday Genius;* Palm Press, publisher of *Longer I Wait, More You Love Me,* and Duke University Press, publisher of *Black Performance Theory*; David Dunton, my agent, for his encouragement; Elizabeth Kendall, Margo Jefferson, Alexandra Chasin, Amy Benson, Patricia Ybarra, Marty Rojas, and Robin Coste Lewis for reading early drafts, kindness, and inspiration; Adrienne

Kennedy for serving as instigator and metaphor, her works remain among my essential texts; Roger D. Hodge for taking the risk of publishing my very first essay; John D'Agata for his enthusiasm and advocacy; Sarah Gorham for her editorial engagement and advice; Derek for Norway; Craig from the corner of my eye; my extended family from coast to coast; my mom, Toni S. Walters, for her courage and endurance; Isaac for providing respite from these questions by asking new ones I would have never dreamed up; and most of all, to Dan Charnas, who is dear and beloved. This work would not have been possible without his support, understanding, patience, and editorial eye. For this and much more, I am so grateful.

Wendy S. Walters is the author of two books of poems, *Troy, Michigan* (Futurepoem, 2014) and *Longer I Wait, More You Love Me* (Palm Press, 2009), as well as the chapbook *Birds of Los Angeles* (Palm Press, 2005). She is a 2011 New York Foundation for the Arts Fellow in Poetry, a Contributing Editor at *The Iowa Review*, and Associate Professor of creative writing and literature at Eugene Lang College of Liberal Arts at The New School in New York City.